The Supreme Court of Canada
Decision on Aboriginal Title

Delgamuukw

commentary by **Stan Persky**
foreword by **Don Ryan**

David Suzuki Foundation

GREYSTONE BOOKS
DOUGLAS & MCINTYRE
VANCOUVER/TORONTO

The books in the David Suzuki Foundation Series explore human impacts on the environment, with an emphasis on finding solutions. The Foundation was established in 1990 to find ways of achieving a balance between social, economic, and ecological needs. The aim of this series is to illuminate the challenges that face us and the possibilities for a sustainable future for us all.

Commentary copyright © 1998 by Stan Persky

98 99 01 02 03 5 4 3 2 1

Greystone Books
A division of Douglas & McIntyre Ltd.
1615 Venables Street
Vancouver, British Columbia
V5L 2H1

The David Suzuki Foundation
219–2211 West 4th Avenue
Vancouver, British Columbia
V6K 4S2

Canadian Cataloguing in Publication Data

Main entry under title:

Delgamuukw

(The David Suzuki Foundation series)
Copublished by: the David Suzuki Foundation.
ISBN 1-55054-657-0

1. Kitksan Indians—Claims. 2. Wet'suwet'en Indians—Claims.
3. Kitksan Indians—Land tenure. 4. Wet'suwet'en Indians—
Land tenure. 5. Kitksan Indians—Land transfers. 6.
Wet'suwet'en Indians—Land transfers. I. Persky, Stan, 1941-
II. David Suzuki Foundation. III. Series.
KEB529.4.D44 1998   346.71104'32'089972   C98-910604-7
KF8208.D44 1998

Cover photograph and cover design by Peter Cocking
Typeset by Brenda and Neil West, BN Typographics West
Printed and bound in Canada by Best Gagne

Printed on 100% recycled paper

The publisher gratefully acknowledges the assistance of the Canada Council and of the British Columbia Ministry of Tourism, Small Business and Culture. The publisher also acknowledges the financial support of the Government of Canada through the Book Publishing Industry Development Program for its publishing activities.

Contents

Foreword

This publication of the Supreme Court of Canada's decision on *Delgamuukw v. British Columbia*, along with Stan Persky's cogent commentary, will be of immense value to all Canadians who wish to understand the implications of this historic judgement.

On the morning of the decision, Thursday, December 11, 1997, Stuart Rush, our counsel, a group of Gitxsan Hereditary Chiefs, and I braved the Ottawa weather and walked over to the Supreme Court of Canada to receive the decision. Stuart and I speculated on the outcome of the case as we walked. A barrister's room had been reserved for us at the court, and the anticipation and the anxiety in the room were high while we waited for the decision. When it was released, our agent handed it to me in the hallway, and I read the header page. I was shocked, surprised, and, more than anything, relieved that this part of the Gitxsan legal strategy was over. I quickly returned to the room to help distribute the decision to our delegation and to review the decision. We didn't have much time to do a detailed analysis of the decision before facing the media, but the immediate reaction in the room was: "It's a victory."

I remembered the talks Herb George, my counterpart with the Wet'suwet'en, and I had while we were preparing for the Supreme Court of Canada. We had decided that if the court ordered a retrial and if we got some movement on title, it would be a major victory for us. We got this and more.

The centrepiece of the *Delgamuukw* trial was our laws, oral histories, songs, crests, dances, social institutions that govern us, language, and notions of land title, along with our own expert witnesses who testified on our behalf. The Supreme Court of Canada acknowledged parts of this world view and ruled oral histories as valid evidence. This is a tentative step by the court, so we need to do more work to gain full recognition of *Delgamuukw*.

After 152 years of saying our rights and title were extinguished, the Province of British Columbia must now come to terms with *Delgamuukw*. Even in the aftermath of the decision, British Columbia and Canada were saying that aboriginal rights and title are just concepts in law and do not exist on the ground. The Gitxsan do not want to be forced to prove our title. The Supreme Court of Canada has already sent a clear signal to British Columbia to say the Gitxsan and Wet'suwet'en have an interest in the land, including governance. The court went on to instruct the parties to reconcile aboriginal title and Crown title through good-faith negotiations. To this end, in early February 1998, the Gitxsan put forward a reconciliation agreement to British Columbia, and the official response is to agree to agree on a reconciliation process. The Gitxsan will do our best to protect the land and the resources that have provided for us since our oral histories began.

'Maas Gaak (Don Ryan)
Chief Negotiator, Gitxsan Treaty Office

Acknowledgements

I'm grateful for *pro bono* legal advice from Phil Bryden, Don Rosenbloom, and Jack MacDonald, none of whom should be charged with any errors of interpretation I may have perpetrated, and I also wish to acknowledge the encouragement to write about the *Delgamuukw* case from my editors at the *Vancouver Sun*—Mike Sasges, Daphne Bramham, and John Cruickshank—and my colleagues at the David Suzuki Foundation—Jim Fulton, Tara Cullis, David Hocking, and David Suzuki.

—Stan Persky

Commentary

In Native Territory

From the moment of its release into the hands of waiting reporters on December 11, 1997, the Supreme Court of Canada's decision on aboriginal title in the case of *Delgamuukw v. British Columbia* was immediately recognized as a landmark judgement. The Court ruled, unanimously and more forcefully than ever before, that Native people in Canada have a unique claim to their traditional lands, that provinces don't have the power to arbitrarily extinguish aboriginal title, and that future courts must accept valid Native oral history as a key ingredient in proving such claims.

The consequences of the decision were clearly reflected in the front page headline of the *Vancouver Sun*, which declared the next morning: "In Historic Judgment, Top Court Strengthens Indian Land Claims." (1) Correspondents deployed from Ottawa to Vancouver to the "grey cedar Gitanmaax Hall" in Hazelton, B.C., recorded the response of heartened aboriginal leaders. (2)

Concluding a series of trials that had begun a full decade earlier, the Supreme Court of Canada unanimously ruled in favour of two groups of Native people—the Gitxsan and Wet'suwet'en —who have lived amid the watersheds of the Bulkley and Skeena Rivers in north central British Columbia for at least several thousand years, according to archeological evidence.

In Hazelton, "a select group huddled in a closed room with the lawyers, reading the judgment as it arrived page by page, on a fax machine...." Moments before the arrival of the decision, "many

1

of the hereditary chiefs who had taken the case to court [years ago] ... filed solemnly into the hall, filling a circle of chairs at the front. Many wore elaborate headdresses decorated with white ermine pelts. The stories of their clans, houses and territories were recorded on their brilliant red and black button blankets." (3)

Gitxsan chief Jim Angus, a school administrator from nearby Kispiox, emerged to speak first. The significance of the ruling, he announced, was that the Supreme Court of Canada had over-turned the earlier judgements of lower B.C. courts, especially that of the trial judge—B.C. Chief Justice Allan McEachern—that aboriginal title did not exist in law. In addition, a new trial was ordered. The news of the decision was "greeted with applause, with drumming, and with a few tears by hundreds who had gathered by 6 a.m. for a community pancake breakfast." (4)

"In a historic judgment," said the *Sun*'s front page story, "Canada's highest court tried to clarify the murky concept of native Indian land rights." Although there was already controversy about the meaning of the decision, reported the paper, the justices not only ordered a new trial but also "ruled on several key issues that arose in the case. Most significantly, they described the nature and scope of 'aboriginal title,' set out the rules for proving its existence, and ruled it is a constitutionally protected right." In addition, the Court said that while aboriginal title may be "infringed," Native people "must be consulted about the use of their traditional lands, and must receive 'fair compensation.'" The Court also said that in future cases, aboriginal oral history ought to carry equal weight with written Canadian history. Finally, the justices ruled that aboriginal title cannot be extinguished by the province. (5)

The evening of the decision, television screens across Canada were filled with the requisite colourful "visuals" of Gitxsan and Wet'suwet'en people, along with appropriate sound bites. "'The power of the blanket' is still very alive, and we're going to carry it forward," said Jim Angus, referring to the stories and songs passed from generation to generation at feast hall ceremonies. Wet'-suwet'en chief Victor Jim reassured non-Native property owners in the region that "our chiefs have always said that we have to live with our neighbours. We're not going to kick anybody off the land." Peter Weeber, the mayor of the predominantly non-Native community of nearby New Hazelton, dismissed more extreme fears about the impact of the decision. "I haven't heard anything . . . that scares me," Weeber said. (6)

Characteristic of the nuanced sentiments of the Gitxsan and Wet'suwet'en that day were the words of Gitxsan spokesperson Ray Jones, who said, "I have mixed emotions today. I am filled with joy and also with remembrance of people who have worked so hard. I remember our Elders who passed on with broken hearts and the words of [B.C.] Chief Justice McEachern in their ears. Today's decision begins to heal the wounds. The Supreme Court of Canada has come out on the side of justice and humanity." (7)

Naturally, not everyone saw the Court's decision in this light. Perhaps the leading critic of the *Delgamuukw* ruling was Melvin H. Smith, a former constitutional adviser and deputy minister in the B.C. provincial government, and the author of *Our Home or Native Land?*, a book opposing aboriginal land claims. Smith would soon pepper the province with letters to the editor, media appearances, and speeches to prominent business groups. (8)

Referring to the Oregon Boundary Treaty of 1846, Smith bitterly claimed, just days after the decision came down, that "the Court has ignored completely what the assertion of British sovereignty over the territory in 1846 really means." (9) Of course, many observers were at odds with Smith's interpretation. Citing Smith's remark, one commentator replied that far from ignoring the assertion of British sovereignty, "in fact, the Supreme Court has at last defined what the 'assertion of sovereignty' means: it means that it was an assertion limited by aboriginal title." (10)

However, Smith's views were echoed by a variety of generally right-wing commentators, from *Globe and Mail* columnist and Reform Party supporter Gordon Gibson to a raucous chorus of "hot-line" radio show hosts, led by a former Social Credit cabinet minister, Rafe Mair, who had contributed a foreword to Smith's book. The leader of the legislative Opposition even suggested that any settlements that might be negotiated should be subject to popular referenda, a notion that was promptly criticized as a recipe for unleashing unchecked emotions and rhetoric.

Yet, curiously, the full effect of the *Delgamuukw* decision didn't hit the general public until months later. When it did, it came in the form of a spectacular, if strangely distorted, newspaper report that, once more, commanded the front page of the *Vancouver Sun*. "B.C. Indian Chiefs Lay Claim to Entire Province, Resources," trumpeted the Monday morning page one headline of the February 2, 1998, issue of the paper, jolting commuters and coffee drinkers out of their reveries. (11)

"B.C.'s native Indians are laying claim to every tree, every rock, every fish and every animal in the province," said the wildly alarmist opening paragraph of Rick Ouston's lead story. "In an unprecedented set of demands, the province's reserve Indians are brandishing a recent Supreme Court of Canada decision they say grants them unfettered control of the entire B.C. land mass, including forests, mines and fish." (12)

As it turned out, Ouston was reporting on a weekend meeting between the First Nations Summit and federal Indian Affairs minister Jane Stewart and her B.C. provincial counterpart, but there was little in what followed to justify the sensational headline or the story's histrionic beginning. In fact, as readers turned the page to get the details, they were soothingly assured by a First Nations Summit press release that "it is not First Nations' intention to bankrupt the economy of the province. Rather, it is our objective to assume our rightful place and to fully participate in the economy and the future of this province." (13) More sanguine souls might read this moderate rhetoric as simply meeting the norms of negotiating talk.

Nonetheless, as an accompanying *Sun* editorial noted, "The silence since the Delgamuukw decision is finally being broken." Rather than focussing exclusively on *Delgamuukw*, the paper urged the signing of a proposed treaty whose principles had already been initialed by governments and the council of the Nisga'a, a Native nation dwelling in the Nass River Valley, just northwest of Gitxsan territory. The Nisga'a's lengthy negotiations on aboriginal rights and title were more advanced than those of any of the more than forty groups involved in a joint treaty process that had been in progress for most of the decade. (14)

Given that silence in British Columbia's public forum is such a rare thing, perhaps we should be grateful for the couple of months of quiet following the *Delgamuukw* decision. Ever since that brief hiatus, airwaves, newspaper pages, and public gatherings have been alive with loud debate on the implications of the Supreme Court's historic decision. The talk has ranged from fond hopes for some form of comanagement of disputed areas of the province to demands for referenda and federally legislated extinguishment of aboriginal title, albeit with compensation.

This last suggestion was proposed by the redoubtable Mel Smith, possibly stung by the claim "that the Delgamuukw decision shows that [his] advice to previous provincial governments was wrong." All Smith would say in response to that claim was a terse "perhaps," before going on to rail at a "distant and cloistered court in Ottawa ... swayed by the sophistry of the Royal Commission on Aboriginal Peoples and its coterie of like-minded academics," who had the temerity to "create new law on the subject out of thin air and thereby cast aside well-established legal and constitutional principles." (15)

Readers will shortly have the opportunity to decide for themselves on the merits or faults of the Supreme Court of Canada decision. Notwithstanding Smith's discovery of the distance between Ottawa and Lotusland, it does seem slightly contemptuous to ignore the presence on the Court of Justice Beverly McLachlin, a leading jurist from British Columbia. Smith, of course, is the same expert who, in the wake of an earlier appeal court decision unfavourable to Native people, reminded citizens that "the law in this province on the subject of aboriginal interest as determined by the Court ... must be the guiding light to settling land claims in this province. To proceed otherwise is to ignore the rule of law and the Constitution." (16) Indeed.

I cite at length such commentary only to give a hint of the depth of feeling that attends these issues. More important, though, is the fact that underlying the *Delgamuukw* decision are several lengthy legal and human stories. Those interested in relatively complete versions of those sagas are referred to the list of further readings at the end of this commentary. Three legal strands need to be briefly mentioned, however, if only because they are extensively discussed in the Supreme Court's *Delgamuukw* decision.

The longest of these legal stories extends from the British Royal Proclamation of 1763 to the Canadian Constitution Act of 1982. It is a story that encompasses an enormous amount of human interaction and suffering, as well as a history of formal relations between governments and Canadian aboriginals that embodies considerable statutory and case law.

More than two hundred years ago, before the Gitxsan and Wet'suwet'en peoples came into contact with European visitors, businessmen and settlers, the Crown proclaimed:

And we do further declare it to be Our Royal Will and Pleasure, for the present as aforesaid, to reserve under our Sovereignty, Protection, and Dominion, for the use of the said Indians, all the Lands and Territories not included within the Limits of Our said Three new Governments, or within the Limits of the Territory granted to the Hudson's Bay Company, as also all the Lands and Territories lying to the Westward of the Sources of the Rivers which fall into the Sea from the West and North West as aforesaid.

As Justice La Forest remarks in *Delgamuukw*, "Although the *Proclamation* is not the sole source of 'aboriginal title' in this country, it bears witness to the British policy towards aboriginal people which was based on respect for their rights to occupy their ancestral lands." (17)

Some two centuries and a great many "saids" and "aforesaids" later, the newly repatriated 1982 Constitution of Canada succinctly declared in section 35(1) that "the existing aboriginal and treaty rights of the aboriginal peoples of Canada are hereby recognized and affirmed." (18) But determining just exactly what those rights are is what brings us to cases such as *Delgamuukw*.

There is a briefer, more localized jurisprudential story as well. As Chief Justice Lamer says at the very beginning of his reasons in *Delgamuukw*, "This appeal is the latest in a series of cases in which it has fallen to this Court to interpret and apply the guarantee of existing aboriginal rights found in s. 35(1) of the *Constitution Act, 1982*. Although that line of decisions ... laid down the jurisprudential framework for s. 35(1), this appeal raises a set of interrelated and novel questions which revolve around a single issue—the nature and scope of the constitutional protection afforded ... to common law aboriginal title." (19)

The "line of decisions" now extending to *Delgamuukw* is importantly foreshadowed by a 1973 Supreme Court case that, as one commentator, Stephen Hume, puts it, "became the symbolic watershed regarding aboriginal title in B.C." It began when Frank Calder, a Nisga'a chief, went to court "seeking a declaration that the tribe still held an unextinguished aboriginal title to its traditional lands. The people of the Nass River had never signed a treaty, had always asserted their sovereignty over their territory, could find no provincial or federal legislation extinguishing title and remained the overwhelming majority in their valley." (20)

In the end, although Calder lost on a technicality in a split decision, the lasting impact of the Court's ruling was its conclusion that aboriginal title did exist in law and that where it was not extinguished it must continue in force. It was the dissenting opinions of the Court that persuaded the Liberal government of the day, led by Prime Minister Pierre Trudeau, to reverse its policy and to begin negotiating land claims in regions of the country—British Columbia, Yukon and the Northwest Territories—where there were no treaties. As Justice La Forest says in *Delgamuukw*, "In my view, the foundation of 'aboriginal title' was succinctly described by [Justice] Judson in *Calder v Attorney-General of British Columbia* (1973)," and then La Forest cites once more an oft-quoted passage from Judson: "The fact is that when the settlers came, the Indians were there, organized in societies and occupying the land as their forefathers had done for centuries. This is what Indian title means." (21)

Finally, amid the strands of legal decision making that led to the Supreme Court's judgement in *Delgamuukw* are the lower court verdicts in this case. Since the initial *Delgamuukw* case is discussed extensively in the next section, only the briefest sketch is required here.

This extraordinary four-year trial was heard by B.C. Supreme Court Justice Allan McEachern from 1987 to 1991. There were

more than 370 days of testimony, some 60-plus witnesses, 23,000
pages of trial transcript, and the expenditure of at least $25 mil-
lion. Justice McEachern's reasons ran to some 400 pages. But the
crux of his decision could be boiled down to a crushing paragraph:
"It is the law that aboriginal rights exist at the 'pleasure of the
Crown,' and they may be extinguished whenever the intention
of the Crown to do so is plain and clear." Justice McEachern
thought that the Crown had clearly and plainly exercised that
"pleasure." "The plaintiffs' claims for aboriginal rights are accordingly dismissed."

Along the way, the trial judge also dismissed all the oral history,
personal memories, and pro-Native anthropological evidence
upon which the Gitxsan and Wet'suwet'en had based their claims.
Justice McEachern, in what one critic described as a "late one
night at the Legion" version of B.C. history, decided that the pre-
historic inhabitants of Gitksan and Wet'suwet'en territory were a
pretty rudimentary lot whose lives, he said—quoting 17th-century
political philosopher Thomas Hobbes—were "nasty, brutish, and
short." (22)

It doesn't take much sympathetic imagination to see why
Native groups were devastated by a brutal decision that had even
Ottawa mandarins at the federal justice department shaking their
heads. The legal bureaucrats weren't the only ones who doubted
that McEachern would have the last word. Hugh Brody, one of
the noted anthropologists who testified at the initial 1987–1991
trial and whose testimony was summarily dismissed by McEachern, presciently wrote in 1988:

It is possible that the legal action brought by the Gitksan and Wet'suwet'en against the Province of British Columbia will result in the Supreme
Court of Canada making a ruling on the whole vexed question of aboriginal
rights in Canada, a ruling that could have many implications for both the
theory and application of inter-cultural relationships in first world countries.
(23)

A decade later, that's exactly what the Supreme Court of
Canada did in *Delgamuukw v. British Columbia.*

Reading *Delgamuukw*

The first question reporters asked newly appointed B.C. Aboriginal Affairs minister Dale Lovick in early March 1998 was "What do you think of *Delgamuukw?*" The new minister admitted that he had yet to read the court's decision. Although Lovick no doubt quickly brought himself up to speed in his portfolio, he wasn't the only one in British Columbia who hadn't perused this important and fascinating booklength legal document, the official title of which is *Delgamuukw v. British Columbia.*

The reason for publishing the Supreme Court of Canada decision on aboriginal title in an unexpurgated, hard-copy, accessible edition is that the judgement merits a wider and more general audience than the legal community. Because court decisions are considered rather forbidding, perhaps a bit of guidance will be useful in making this crucial legal text more understandable to a general readership.

Readers who don't make a habit of thumbing through court documents will be pleasantly surprised, I think, to find that the "reasons for judgement," as they are known, are eminently readable and offered in a straightforwardly logical order. Admittedly, at first sight, the language of legal reasoning can appear a bit daunting. In short order, however, a seemingly mysterious phrase, such as "The leading statement of this principle can be found in *Stein v the Ship 'Kathy K'*, [1976] 2 S.C.R. 802, per Ritchie J., at p. 808 ...", translates into "Justice Ritchie made an important statement in a 1976 case involving a person named Stein and a vessel named the *Kathy K*, a report of which can be found in volume 2 of the Supreme Court Reports, beginning on page 802. Justice Ritchie's remark is on page 808 and says the following...." Legal readers who are familiar with this form of referencing are thus able to rush off to their nearest law library or to log on to the appropriate Internet website and locate the case; general readers, presumably, will simply pass over this bit of shorthand.

Previous decisions are frequently referred to, partly because the courts are intended, almost by definition, to be conservative. Far from creating new law "out of thin air," as some critics charge, what's fascinating, both to new and experienced readers of high court judgements, is to see firsthand how justices "work" a piece of law, nodding to earlier interpretations and precedents, and yet attempting to come to terms with a changing societal sense of what is just in a particular instance.

Before the reader gets to the actual reasons of the justices—in *Delgamuukw* the principal judgement is written by Chief Justice Antonio Lamer, who has also been the author of most recent decisions concerning aboriginal rights—there is a good bit of prefatory material, known as the "headnotes," that provides a summary of what the Court decided.

The first thing we learn is who is involved in the case. In this instance, it's a man named Delgamuukw, also known as Earl Muldoe, and a great many other members and representatives of Gitxsan and Wet'suwet'en "Houses." They are known as the "appellants," and they are "appealing," or seeking a reversal of, a previous decision of the Court of Appeal for British Columbia. They are suing "Her Majesty the Queen in Right of the Province of British Columbia," and the Attorney General of Canada, who are known as the "respondents." Although the case is formally filed as *Delgamuukw v. British Columbia,* sometimes people refer to the case as *Delgamuukw v. R.,* where "*R.*" is shorthand for "Regina," referring to the Queen. In addition, there is a list of other parties, ranging from the First Nations Summit to Alcan Aluminum Ltd., who have a pressing interest in the case and something they want to say to the Court. These latter parties are known as "interveners."

After the roster of the participants, including a list of the justices who heard the case, there's an indexical cataloguing of the points of law affected by the decision, such as "Constitutional law—Aboriginal rights—Aboriginal land title—Evidence—Oral history and native law and tradition," and so on. This is followed by a brief summary of the case in which the Gitxsan and Wet'-suwet'en people are laying claim to various portions of 58,000 square kilometres of land in British Columbia, and a brief account of the decisions by the lower courts, which are now being appealed. This summary includes a set of the principal issues that the Supreme Court of Canada decided to take up.

The five main issues in *Delgamukkw* are:

(1) Is the Court able to decide on the claims for aboriginal title and self-government? This first issue is a technical question in which the Court has to determine whether the way in which the case was put forward—known in legal language as the "pleadings"—makes it impossible to rule on the issues of substance. If a party to a case changes—even slightly—what it asks the courts to decide from what it asked previous and lower courts to rule on, a change in pleadings is said to occur, and this change may prevent the court now hearing the case from deciding all aspects of the case.

(2) What is the ability of this Court to interfere with the factual findings made by the trial judge of the Court of Appeal for British Columbia? This is one of the critical issues of *Delgamuukw*. Although appeal courts routinely decide whether trial judges made errors of law, it's unusual for higher courts to determine whether the trial judge's decision about the facts of the case were in error.

(3) What is the content of aboriginal title, how is it protected by section 35(1) of the Canadian Constitution, and what is required for its proof?

(4) Did the appellants make a substantial claim for self-government over the land they were claiming? That is, if there is aboriginal title, then how is the land for which title is claimed going to be governed, and who is going to govern it? The Court is here examining whether the appellants have laid out a sufficient case for the Court to be able to decide this contentious issue at this time.

(5) Does the province have the power to extinguish aboriginal rights?

It's then tersely reported that the Court "held" (or decided) that "the appeal should be allowed in part." The formal finding is followed by an extended paraphrased summary of the court's reasoning on each of the questions before it. The prefatory material concludes with a bibliography of cases, laws, and authors cited in the justices' reasons.

After a brief re-announcement of the case and a listing of the legal participants involved in it, the "reasons for judgement," or actual words of the justices, then appear in a series of 209 numbered paragraphs.

In *Delgamuukw*, where there is no dissent to a unanimous judgement, attention focusses on the main set of reasons, occupying some 90 per cent of the decision, written by Chief Justice Antonio Lamer, with Justices Cory and Major agreeing. There is also a second, briefer set of reasons, offered by Justice La Forest, with Justice L'Heureux-Dubé concurring, that agrees with the decision to allow the appeal but takes a somewhat different route to get to that conclusion.

Chief Justice Lamer's opinion is set out in a logical jurisprudential format that, successively, provides a brief introduction to the case the Court is considering, an account of the "facts," a careful review of previous lower court judgements, a setting out of the issues, and a lengthy "analysis," followed by conclusions and the disposition of the case. The heart of the decision is, of course, the analysis in which Chief Justice Lamer's interpretations establish our present understanding of the law.

What Did the Court Decide?

In the simplest sense, what the Supreme Court of Canada decided on December 11, 1997, in *Delgamuukw* was to allow, in part, the appeal of the Gitxsan and Wet'suwet'en people. The meaning of allowing the appeal is that previous lower court decisions in the case are overturned and a new trial, to be held within the framework of the Supreme Court's interpretation of crucial issues, is ordered.

In formally ordering a new trial, Chief Justice Lamer is not encouraging the parties to go back to court. As he says, "This litigation has been both long and expensive, not only in economic but in human terms as well. By ordering a new trial, I do not necessarily encourage the parties to proceed to litigation and to settle their dispute through the courts." As Lamer had noted in a previous case, s. 35(1) of the Constitution "provides a solid constitutional base upon which subsequent negotiations can take place." He adds, "Ultimately, it is through negotiated settlements, with good faith and give and take on all sides, reinforced by the

judgements of this Court, that we will achieve ... 'the reconciliation of the pre-existence of aboriginal societies with the sovereignty of the Crown.' Let us face it, we are all here to stay." (24)
Technically speaking, the Court could have done no more than
order a new trial. "This appeal demands, however," says Lamer,
"that the Court now explore and elucidate the implications of the
constitutionalization of aboriginal title. The first is the specific
content of aboriginal title, a question which this Court has not yet
definitively addressed.... The second is the related question of the
test for the proof of title.... This appeal also raises an important
practical problem relevant to the proof of aboriginal title which is
endemic to aboriginal rights litigation generally—the treatment of
the oral histories of Canada's aboriginal peoples by the courts." (25)
The two most important matters that the Court decided in
Delgamuukw are the issues Lamer cites above. To greatly simplify
these issues, the Court decided that (1) *stories matter,* and (2) not
only is aboriginal title recognized in both common and constitutional law, but it has specific content and implications. The phrase
"stories matter" refers to the Court's precedent-establishing decision that aboriginal oral histories must be given significant weight
in any subsequent legal proceedings. Although it is the decision
on aboriginal title that will have the most practical impact on
future relationships in British Columbia, I'm deeply struck, as
have been other observers, by the Court's recognition of aboriginal oral history. This recognition has practical consequences, since
such histories are the primary means by which Native nations can
prove their claims to aboriginal title. But at a deeper level, what I
read in the Court's decision on oral history is a more profound
effort to reconcile how different peoples with different cultural
traditions see the world. Accordingly, it is upon this aspect of the
Court's decision that I want to focus.

Chief Justice Lamer begins his own "story" of the case by
observing that the court action was commenced by Gitxsan and
Wet'suwet'en hereditary chiefs who claimed various portions of
58,000 square kilometres in British Columbia. He notes that
"their claim was originally for 'ownership' and 'jurisdiction' over
it," but that at this Court, the original claim "was transformed

into, primarily, a claim for aboriginal title over the land in question." (26) The changed character of the claim will have (see below) a technical consequence for the Court's decision.

The Gitxsan, Lamer reports, consist of some five thousand people who live in the area of the Skeena, Nass and Babine River watersheds, while the Wet'suwet'en are approximately two thousand people who live in the neighbouring watersheds of the Bulkley and other nearby river systems. "There was archeological evidence," accepted by trial judge McEachern, "that there was some form of human habitation in the territory and its surrounding areas from 3500 to 6000 years ago, and intense occupation of the Hagwilget Canyon site (near Hazelton), prior to about 4000 to 3500 years ago," Lamer writes. (27)

By way of proving that they occupied their territories, and in addition to totem poles, house crests and other distinctive regalia, "the Gitksan houses have an 'adaawk' which is a collection of sacred oral tradition about their ancestors, histories and territories. The Wet'suwet'en each have a 'kungax' which is a spiritual song or dance or performance which ties them to their land.... The most significant evidence of spiritual connection between the Houses and their territory is a feast hall. This is where the Gitksan and Wet'suwet'en people tell and re-tell their stories and identify their territories to remind themselves of the sacred connection that they have with their lands." (28) It is the treatment of the *adaawk* and *kungax*, much of which was entered as evidence at the initial trial, that is at the centre of Chief Justice Lamer's concern.

That concern takes the form of a legal question: "What is the ability of this Court to interfere with the factual findings made by the trial judge?" Lamer immediately makes it clear that this is an unusual question. "As a general rule, this Court has been extremely reluctant to interfere with the findings of fact made at trial, especially when those findings of fact are based on an assessment of the testimony and credibility of witnesses. Unless there is a 'palpable and overriding error,' appellate courts should not substitute their own findings of fact for those of the trial judge." (29) The reason underlying that general rule is to protect the autonomy and integrity of the trial process. That is, it's recognized that the trial judge, who is in direct contact with the mass of evidence, is usually in the best position to make findings of fact. However, "while accepting the general principle of non-interference, this Court has also identified specific situations in which an appeal court can interfere with a finding of fact," one of which is "the failure of a trial court to appreciate the evidentiary difficulties inherent in adjudicating aboriginal claims." In an earlier decision, but one that came after trial judge McEachern's 1991 decision, Chief Justice Lamer wrote:

A court should approach the rules of evidence, and interpret the evidence that exists, with a consciousness of the special nature of aboriginal claims, and of the evidentiary difficulties in proving a right which originates in times where there were no written records. . . . The courts must not undervalue the evidence presented by aboriginal claimants simply because that evidence does not conform precisely with the evidentiary standards that would be applied in, for example, a private law torts case [a case involving a breach of duty leading to liability of damages]. (30)

The fact that Lamer spelled out this interpretation of weighing evidence after McEachern's original *Delgamuukw* ruling allows for a bit of fortuitous face-saving. Lamer will be able to note that the trial judge didn't have the "benefit" of the Supreme Court's later wisdom on the matter and, therefore, can be partially excused for whatever errors he made.

Lamer continues, "The justification for this special approach can be found in the nature of aboriginal rights themselves." Those rights are aimed at reconciling the prior occupation of North America by distinct aboriginal societies with the assertion of Crown sovereignty over Canadian territory. Accordingly, "a court must take into account the perspective of the aboriginal people." In other words, says Lamer, aboriginal rights "demand a unique approach to the treatment of evidence which accords due weight to the perspective of aboriginal peoples." Lamer isn't saying that anything that aboriginals say must be accepted; rather the accommodation of the Native perspective "must be done in a manner which does not strain 'the Canadian legal and constitutional structure.'" (31)

Having established that courts must "come to terms with the oral histories of aboriginal societies, which, for many aboriginal nations, are the only record of their past," Lamer now turns to the nature of aboriginal oral history itself. Although some critics chafed at its "sophistry," Lamer cites the 1996 *Report of the Royal Commission on Aboriginal Peoples* for providing "a useful and informative description of aboriginal oral history."

The Royal Commission said that "the aboriginal tradition in the recording of history is neither linear nor steeped" in non-Native notions of social progress. "Nor is it usually human centred in the same way as anything in the Western scientific tradition, for it does not assume that human beings are anything more than one—and not necessarily the most important—element in the natural order of the universe." Native oral tradition, the Royal Commission noted, "is less focussed on establishing objective truth and assumes that the teller of the story is so much a part of the event being described that it would be arrogant to presume to classify or categorise the event exactly or for all time." (32)

Lamer recognizes that this poetic, almost ontological, account of Native oral history poses "difficulties" for traditional courtroom treatment of evidence. "Notwithstanding these challenges," Lamer insists, "the laws of evidence must be adopted in order that this type of evidence can be accommodated and placed on an equal footing with the types of historical evidence that courts are familiar with, which largely consists of historical documents." Otherwise, an "impossible burden of proof" would be put on peoples who did not have written records, which would "render nugatory" any rights that they might have. (33) In so declaring that Native oral history should be placed "on an equal footing" with other types of evidence, the Supreme Court established a new interpretation of the law's handling of evidence.

Having eloquently prepared the ground, Lamer returns to the issue of interfering with the trial judge's finding of facts. He conducts an extended consideration of the application of the principles he's laid down, devoting particular attention to the *adaawk* and *kungax,* as well as "recollections of aboriginal life" and "territorial affidavits," each of which occasions a review of Justice McEachern's findings of fact.

Of particular importance are the *adaawk* and *kungax*—"oral histories of a special kind," and obviously of "integral importance to the distinctive cultures of the appellant nations." Although McEachern admitted this material, "the trial judge, however, went on to give these oral histories no independent weight at all.... He discounted the *adaawk* and *kungax* because they were not 'literally true,' confounded 'what is fact and what is belief,' 'included some material which might be classified as mythology,' and projected a 'romantic view' of the history of the appellants...." (34)

"In summary, the trial judge gave no independent weight to these special oral histories, because they did not accurately convey historical truth, because knowledge about those oral histories was confined to the communities whose histories they were, and because oral histories were insufficiently detailed," Lamer continues. "However, these are features to a greater or lesser extent, of all oral histories, not just the *adaawk* and *kungax.* The implication of the trial judge's reasoning is that oral histories should never be given any independent weight and are only useful as confirmatory evidence in aboriginal rights litigation. I fear that if this reasoning were followed, the oral histories of aboriginal peoples would be consistently and systematically undervalued by the Canadian legal system." (35)

This is the "palpable and overriding" error in Justice McEachern's finding of facts, the error that justifies an unusual interference on the part of the Supreme Court of Canada. "The trial judge's treatment of the various kinds of oral histories did not satisfy the principles" that the Court has laid down. "These errors are particularly worrisome because oral histories were of critical importance to the appellants' case.... Had the trial judge assessed the oral histories correctly, his conclusions on these issues of fact might have been very different." (36)

The language of the overruling of the trial judge is subtle, but there is no mistaking how thoroughly McEachern's decision is being shredded. "In the circumstances, the factual findings cannot stand," Lamer rules. He doesn't propose that the Supreme Court of Canada make new factual findings, however. Rather, "a new trial is warranted." (37)

In any case, earlier in Lamer's reasons, when considering whether the form of the "pleadings" prevented the Court from entertaining claims for aboriginal title and self-government, the Chief Justice, on technical grounds, had already disposed of the notion of settling all matters in this decision. The technical issue was that the original claim had been altered in the appeal. Claims for ownership and jurisdiction had been replaced with claims for aboriginal title and self-government, and second, individual house claims had been amalgamated into two communal claims. This "defect" in the pleadings "prevents the Court from considering the merits of this appeal," and the correct remedy for the defects in the pleadings is a new trial. Of course, as has already become clear in the discussion of the trial judge's errors in findings of fact, there were other, more substantial, reasons for ordering a new trial.

I'll deal more briefly with the other major finding in *Delga-muukw,* namely, the Court's definition of the content of the notion of aboriginal title. Chief Justice Lamer insists that aborig-inal title is *sui generis,* or "in a class of its own." Which is also to say—as high courts have been saying ever since *Calder* in 1973 —that there really is such a thing as aboriginal title. In a sense, that reiteration of its existence is as important as anything else in the definition of content, since opponents of aboriginal claims all too frequently try to forget that its existence must have some consequential meaning in the real world.

"I believe that all of the parties have characterized the content of aboriginal title incorrectly," Lamer boldly begins.

The appellants argue that aboriginal title is tantamount to an inalienable fee simple. . . . The respondents offer two alternative formulations: first, that abo-riginal title is no more than a bundle of rights to engage in activities which are themselves aboriginal rights recognized by s. 35(1) . . . and second, that aboriginal title, at most, encompasses the right to exclusive use and occupa-tion of land in order to engage in those activities which are aboriginal rights themselves. (38)

Lamer continues: "The content of aboriginal title, in fact, lies somewhere in between these positions. Aboriginal title is a right in land and, as such, is more than the rights to engage in specific activities which may themselves be aboriginal rights." Further, such title "confers the right to use land for a variety of activities, not all of which need be aspects of practices, customs and traditions which are integral to the distinctive cultures of aboriginal societies." (39) Which is to say, aboriginal title isn't outright "ownership" of anything, but it is more than the right to continue the traditional practice of, say, hunting moose in a particular territory. And the practices and customs that are included in the exercise of aboriginal title are, to put it colloquially, a lot more than singing, dancing, hunting, and hanging out. They may well include considerable rights to the resources of the territory covered by title.

Although Lamer's definition of the content of aboriginal title is clearer than anything heretofore in Canadian jurisprudence, it is not as clear-cut as the Chief Justice's remarks about oral history. Nonetheless, Lamer recognizes that aboriginal title is a communal form of relationship to the land, and that such lands cannot be used, either by Natives or non-Natives, in such a way as to destroy the way of life of Native people.

In addition to finding that aboriginal title is a right protected by the constitution, Lamer also sets out the test for proof of aboriginal title. "In order to make out a claim for aboriginal title, the aboriginal group asserting title must satisfy the following criteria: (i) the land must have been occupied prior to sovereignty, (ii) if present occupation is relied on as proof of occupation presovereignty, there must be a continuity between present and presovereignty occupation, and (iii) at sovereignty, that occupation must have been exclusive." (40) Lamer notes that "British sovereignty over British Columbia was conclusively established by the *Oregon Boundary Treaty* of 1846." Previously he noted that "aboriginal title is a burden on the Crown's underlying title.... Because it does not make sense to speak of a burden on underlying title before that title existed, aboriginal title crystallized at the time sovereignty was asserted." (41) Again, all of the foregoing is a reiteration that something, namely, aboriginal title, exists and persists, and is a rejection of all sorts of theories that seek to suggest that such title was extinguished either by law or some form of conquest.

Finally, Chief Justice Lamer, while having noted that aboriginal title is an "underlying burden" on Crown title, nonetheless also rules that "the aboriginal rights recognized and affirmed by s. 35(1), including aboriginal title, are not absolute. Those rights may be infringed, both by the federal and provincial governments." (42) However, any "infringement" must be justified. Lamer then sets out the rules for justifying an infringement on aboriginal title.

The rules, based on earlier decisions about aboriginal rights, are fairly detailed, but in the end, the Chief Justice sets forth a broad notion of grounds for infringement:

In my opinion, the development of agriculture, forestry, mining, and hydro-electric power, the general economic development of the interior of British Columbia, protection of the environment or endangered species, the building of infrastructure and the settlement of foreign populations to support those aims, are the kinds of objectives that ... can justify the infringement of aboriginal title. Whether a particular measure or government act can be explained by reference to one of those objectives, however, is ultimately a question of fact that will have to be examined on a case-by-case basis. (43)

Since infringement can be justified by a notion as general as "economic development" of the province, it seems to me that criticisms of the judgement as creating intolerable uncertainty for potential investment are overstated.

It's true, however, that even if infringement can be justified, there are some restraints on infringement itself. For example, "There is always a duty of consultation. Whether the aboriginal group has been consulted is relevant to determining whether the infringement of aboriginal title is justified.... In most cases, it will be significantly deeper than mere consultation.... In keeping with the duty of honor and good faith on the Crown, fair compensation will ordinarily be required when aboriginal title is infringed." (44)

Lamer concedes that he's leaving many difficult questions to "another day." While ruling that the provincial government neither has extinguished nor is capable of extinguishing aboriginal title, the Court puts aside the issues of both self-government and levels of possible compensation. At the end, Chief Justice Lamer urges negotiation as the appropriate form of reconciliation and reminds us that "we are all here to stay," which is to say that we ought to figure out a way of living together.

In the months immediately following the Court's decision, there was, expectedly, a good deal of speculation and a considerable amount of behind-the-scenes legal pondering of the decision's practical meaning. There was general agreement that at the very least, *Delgamuukw* strengthens the negotiating position of aboriginal people at the bargaining table. There was also a view that insofar as *Delgamuukw* mandates more of a comanagement approach to land and resources, it will likely prove beneficial to the resolution of ecological problems. British Columbians are indirectly encouraged by the decision, it seems to me, to exercise more care with the earth. Of course, that may be fanciful imagining on my part, but nonetheless, there is little doubt that the Court's rebalancing of relations in the province will further normalize the practice of close scrutiny of land use.

By spring 1998, there were signs that *Delgamuukw* would also encourage clearer demands and even court actions seeking injunctive relief against proposed projects such as logging, road building, and mining. On the other side, critic Mel Smith was telling the Vancouver Board of Trade in apocalyptic tones that "British Columbia today is in a state of crisis unlike anything it has faced in its 127 years within the Canadian federation." (45) Here, I would offer a note of caution. Obviously, any major Supreme Court of Canada decision will ignite enthusiasms and resentments. Nonetheless, I think there are good reasons for prudence on the part of all parties.

Delgamuukw is not the final word on "what it all means." It is not even absolutely clear how we ought to interpret portions of *Delgamuukw*, especially those concerning aboriginal title, infringement, consultation, and compensation. Clearly, it's the Court's intention to encourage negotiated settlement rather than further litigation. Those who insist on litigation may discover that courts will not read *Delgamuukw* as they do and may find themselves further ensnared in a very long process. Even though there may be a presumption of aboriginal title in many cases, courts may decide that where proof of title has yet to be established—which is to say, almost everywhere in British Columbia—hard-and-fast rulings should be put off and narrow technical decisions may be appropriate.

This isn't a time for bitter critics or hotheaded enthusiasts. Although moderation is never the most entertaining counsel to offer, it's often, in the long run, the most valuable.

NOTE: "Gitxsan" is now the preferred spelling of "Gitksan," which is the spelling used throughout *Delgamuukw v. British Columbia.*

Notes

1. *Vancouver Sun,* December 12, 1997, p. A1.
2. Ken McQueen, "Gitxsan History Set Right," *Vancouver Sun,* December 12, 1997, p. A14.
3. Ibid.
4. Ibid.
5. Stewart Bell, Peter O'Neil and Jim Beatty, "In Historic Judgment ...", *Vancouver Sun,* December 12, 1997, p. A1.
6. Loc. cit., McQueen, p. A14.
7. Cited in Dara Culhane, *The Pleasure of the Crown: Anthropology, Law and First Nations* (Vancouver: Talon Books, 1998), p. 360.
8. Melvin H. Smith, *Our Home or Native Land?: What Governments' Aboriginal Policy Is Doing to Canada* (Victoria: Crown Western, 1995).
9. Melvin H. Smith, "What the court ignored in *Delgamuukw,*" *Globe and Mail,* January 7, 1998.
10. Stan Persky, "Settlement of B.C. Was Actually a Resettlement," *Vancouver Sun,* January 16, 1998, p. A19.
11. *Vancouver Sun,* February 2, 1998, p. A1.
12. Rick Ouston, "B.C. Indian Chiefs Lay Claim to Entire Province, Resources," *Vancouver Sun,* February 2, 1998, p. A1.
13. Ibid.
14. "Nisga'a Negotiators Are on Right Road," *Vancouver Sun,* February 2, 1998, p. A10.
15. Melvin H. Smith, "Legislation only hope of settling native land claims," *Vancouver Sun,* March 25, 1998, p. A19.
16. Loc. cit., Melvin H. Smith, *Our Home or Native Land?* p. 141.
17. *Delgamuukw v. British Columbia,* para. 200.
18. R. I. Cheffins and P. A. Johnson, *The Revised Canadian Constitution* (Whitby, Ont.: McGraw-Hill Ryerson, 1986), p. 223.

19. Loc. cit., *Delgamuukw*, para. 1.
20. Stephen Hume, "Dancing toward Delgamuukw," *Vancouver Sun*, April 11, 1998, p. G6.
21. Loc. cit., *Delgamuukw*, para. 189.
22. Loc. cit., Dara Culhane, *The Pleasure of the Crown*, p. 31.
23. Hugh Brody, *Maps and Dreams* (Vancouver: Douglas & McIntyre, 1988), p. xii.
24. Loc. cit., *Delgamuukw*, para. 186.
25. Ibid., paras. 2 and 3.
26. Ibid., para. 7.
27. Ibid., paras. 7–10.
28. Ibid., paras. 13 and 14.
29. Ibid., para. 78.
30. Ibid., para. 80.
31. Ibid., paras. 81 and 82.
32. Ibid., para. 85. Also, cf. Stan Persky, "There's nothing academic any more about unravelling native oral history," *Vancouver Sun*, March 6, 1998.
33. Ibid., para. 87.
34. Ibid., paras. 96 and 97.
35. Ibid., para. 98.
36. Ibid., para. 107.
37. Ibid., para. 108.
38. Ibid., para. 110.
39. Ibid., para. 111.
40. Ibid., para. 143.
41. Ibid., para. 145.
42. Ibid., para. 160.
43. Ibid., para. 165.
44. Ibid., paras. 168 and 169.
45. Cited, with approval, by Trevor Lautens, "How to make Indian land claims go away," *Vancouver Sun*, February 28, 1998, p. A23.

Further Reading
Asch, Michael, ed. *Aboriginal and Treaty Rights in Canada: Essays on Law, Equality, and Respect for Difference* (Vancouver: University of British Columbia Press, 1997). This informative collection contains Kent McNeil's essay, "The Meaning of Aboriginal Title," which is repeatedly cited by Chief Justice Lamer in *Delgamuukw*.
Brody, Hugh. *Maps and Dreams: Indians and the British Columbia Frontier* (Vancouver: Douglas & McIntyre, 1988). A new edition of a noted anthropologist's 1981 account of aboriginal people in northeastern British Columbia that takes seriously the cosmological conceptions of the people

Brody is visiting, as well as providing a scholarly commentary on the history, politics, and social conditions of the region.

Culhane, Dara. *The Pleasure of the Crown: Anthropology, Law and First Nations* (Vancouver: Talon Books, 1998). A detailed, critical account of Justice McEachern's decision in the initial *Delgamuukw* trial, as well as a broad critique of the issue of how the Crown acquired title to aboriginal territories.

Glavin, Terry. *A Death Feast in Dimlahamid* (Vancouver: New Star, 1998). A new edition of Glavin's marvellous 1990 narrative about the lives of the Gitksan people, containing a new chapter discussing *Delgamuukw*.

Harris, Cole. *The Resettlement of British Columbia: Essays on Colonialism and Geographical Change* (Vancouver: University of British Columbia Press, 1997). A historical geographer's perceptive essays on aspects of the "resettlement" of a territory already settled by Native peoples.

McKee, Christopher. *Treaty Talks in British Columbia: Negotiating a Mutually Beneficial Future* (Vancouver: University of British Columbia Press, 1996). A political scientist's account of the development of treaty negotiations in the province.

Smith, Melvin H. *Our Home or Native Land?: What Governments' Aboriginal Policy Is Doing to Canada* (Victoria: Crown Western, 1995). A tendentious presentation of the case against aboriginal rights.

DELGAMUUKW v. BRITISH COLUMBIA
[1997] 3 S.C.R. 1010

Delgamuukw, also known as Earl Muldoe, suing on his own behalf and on behalf of all the members of the Houses of Delgamuukw and Haaxw (and others suing on their own behalf and on behalf of thirty-eight Gitksan Houses and twelve Wet'suwet'en Houses as shown in Schedule 1) *Appellants/Respondents on the cross-appeal*

v.

Her Majesty The Queen in Right of the Province of British Columbia *Respondent/Appellant on the cross-appeal* and The Attorney General of Canada *Respondent*

and

The First Nations Summit, the Musqueam Nation *et al.* (as shown in Schedule 2), the Westbank First Nation, the B.C. Cattlemen's Association *et al.* (as shown in Schedule 3), Skeena Cellulose Inc., Alcan Aluminum Ltd. *Interveners*

Indexed as: Delgamuukw v. British Columbia

File No.: 23799.

1997: June 16, 17; 1997: December 11.

Present: Lamer C.J. and La Forest, L'Heureux-Dubé, Sopinka, Cory, McLachlin and Major JJ.

ON APPEAL FROM THE COURT OF APPEAL FOR BRITISH COLUMBIA

*Constitutional law—Aboriginal rights—Aboriginal land title—
Claim made for large tract—Content of aboriginal title—How
aboriginal title protected by s. 35(1) of Constitution Act, 1982—What
required to prove aboriginal title—Whether claim to self-government
made out—Whether province could extinguish aboriginal rights after
1871, either under own jurisdiction or through the operation of s. 88 of
the Indian Act (incorporating provincial laws of general application by
reference)—Constitution Act, 1982, s. 35(1)—Indian Act, R.S.C., 1985,
c. I-5, s. 88.*

*Constitutional law—Aboriginal rights—Aboriginal land title—
Evidence—Oral history and native law and tradition—Weight to be
given evidence—Ability of Court to interfere with trial judge's factual
findings.*

*Courts—Procedure—Land claims—Aboriginal title and self-
government—Claim altered but no formal amendments to pleadings
made—Whether pleadings precluded the Court from entertaining
claims.*

The appellants, all Gitksan or Wet'suwet'en hereditary chiefs,
both individually and on behalf of their "Houses", claimed separate portions of 58,000 square kilometres in British Columbia. For
the purpose of the claim, this area was divided into 133 individual
territories, claimed by the 71 Houses. This represents all of the
Wet'suwet'en people, and all but 12 of the Gitksan Houses. Their
claim was originally for "ownership" of the territory and "jurisdiction" over it. (At this Court, this was transformed into, primarily,
a claim for aboriginal title over the land in question.) British
Columbia counterclaimed for a declaration that the appellants
have no right or interest in and to the territory or alternatively,
that the appellants' cause of action ought to be for compensation
from the Government of Canada.

At trial, the appellants' claim was based on their historical use
and "ownership" of one or more of the territories. In addition, the
Gitksan Houses have an "adaawk" which is a collection of sacred
oral tradition about their ancestors, histories and territories. The

Wet'suwet'en each have a "kungax" which is a spiritual song or dance or performance which ties them to their land. Both of these were entered as evidence on behalf of the appellants. The most significant evidence of spiritual connection between the Houses and their territory was a feast hall where the Gitksan and Wet'-suwet'en people tell and retell their stories and identify their territories to remind themselves of the sacred connection that they have with their lands. The feast has a ceremonial purpose but is also used for making important decisions.

The trial judge did not accept the appellants' evidence of oral history of attachment to the land. He dismissed the action against Canada, dismissed the plaintiffs' claims for ownership and jurisdiction and for aboriginal rights in the territory, granted a declaration that the plaintiffs were entitled to use unoccupied or vacant land subject to the general law of the province, dismissed the claim for damages and dismissed the province's counterclaim. No order for costs was made. On appeal, the original claim was altered in two different ways. First, the claims for ownership and jurisdiction were replaced with claims for aboriginal title and self-government, respectively. Second, the individual claims by each House were amalgamated into two communal claims, one advanced on behalf of each nation. There were no formal amendments to the pleadings to this effect. The appeal was dismissed by a majority of the Court of Appeal.

The principal issues on the appeal, some of which raised a number of sub-issues, were as follows: (1) whether the pleadings precluded the Court from entertaining claims for aboriginal title and self-government; (2) what was the ability of this Court to interfere with the factual findings made by the trial judge; (3) what is the content of aboriginal title, how is it protected by s. 35(1) of the *Constitution Act, 1982*, and what is required for its proof; (4) whether the appellants made out a claim to self-government; and, (5) whether the province had the power to extinguish aboriginal rights after 1871, either under its own jurisdiction or through the operation of s. 88 of the *Indian Act*.

Held: The appeal should be allowed in part and the cross-appeal should be dismissed.

Whether the Claims Were Properly Before the Court

Per Lamer C.J. and Cory, McLachlin, and Major JJ.: The claims were properly before the Court. Although the pleadings were not formally amended, the trial judge did allow a *de facto* amendment to permit a claim for aboriginal rights other than ownership and jurisdiction. The respondents did not appeal this *de facto* amendment and the trial judge's decision on this point must accordingly stand.

No amendment was made with respect to the amalgamation of the individual claims brought by the individual Gitksan and Wet'-suwet'en Houses into two collective claims, one by each nation, for aboriginal title and self-government. The collective claims were simply not in issue at trial and to frame the case on appeal in a different manner would retroactively deny the respondents the opportunity to know the appellants' case.

A new trial is necessary. First, the defect in the pleadings prevented the Court from considering the merits of this appeal. The parties at a new trial would decide whether any amendment was necessary to make the pleadings conform with the other evidence. Then, too, appellate courts, absent a palpable and overriding error, should not substitute their own findings of fact even when the trial judge misapprehended the law which was applied to those facts. Appellate intervention is warranted, however, when the trial court fails to appreciate the evidentiary difficulties inherent in adjudicating aboriginal claims when applying the rules of evidence and interpreting the evidence before it.

Per La Forest and L'Heureux-Dubé JJ.: The amalgamation of the appellants' individual claims technically prevents a consideration of the merits. However, there is a more substantive problem with the pleadings. The appellants sought a declaration of "aboriginal title" but attempted, in essence, to prove that they had complete control over the territory. It follows that what the appellants sought by way of declaration and what they set out to prove by way of the evidence were two different matters. A new trial should be ordered.

McLachlin J. was in substantial agreement.

The Ability of the Court to Interfere with the Trial Judge's Factual Findings

Per Lamer C.J. and Cory, McLachlin and Major JJ.: The factual findings made at trial could not stand because the trial judge's treatment of the various kinds of oral histories did not satisfy the principles laid down in *R. v. Van der Peet*. The oral histories were used in an attempt to establish occupation and use of the disputed territory which is an essential requirement for aboriginal title. The trial judge refused to admit or gave no independent weight to these oral histories and then concluded that the appellants had not demonstrated the requisite degree of occupation for "ownership". Had the oral histories been correctly assessed, the conclusions on these issues of fact might have been very different.

The Content of Aboriginal Title, How It Is Protected by s. 35(1) of the Constitution Act, 1982, and the Requirements Necessary to Prove It

Per Lamer C.J. and Cory, McLachlin and Major JJ.: Aboriginal title encompasses the right to exclusive use and occupation of the land held pursuant to that title for a variety of purposes, which need not be aspects of those aboriginal practices, customs and traditions which are integral to distinctive aboriginal cultures. The protected uses must not be irreconcilable with the nature of the group's attachment to that land.

Aboriginal title is *sui generis*, and so distinguished from other proprietary interests, and characterized by several dimensions. It is inalienable and cannot be transferred, sold or surrendered to anyone other than the Crown. Another dimension of aboriginal title is its sources: its recognition by the *Royal Proclamation, 1763* and the relationship between the common law which recognizes occupation as proof of possession and systems of aboriginal law pre-existing assertion of British sovereignty. Finally, aboriginal title is held communally.

The exclusive right to use the land is not restricted to the right to engage in activities which are aspects of aboriginal practices, customs and traditions integral to the claimant group's distinctive aboriginal culture. Canadian jurisprudence on aboriginal title frames the "right to occupy and possess" in broad terms and, significantly, is not qualified by the restriction that use be tied to practice, custom or tradition. The nature of the Indian interest in reserve land which has been found to be the same as the interest in tribal lands is very broad and incorporates present-day needs. Finally, aboriginal title encompasses mineral rights and lands held pursuant to aboriginal title should be capable of exploitation. Such a use is certainly not a traditional one.

The content of aboriginal title contains an inherent limit in that lands so held cannot be used in a manner that is irreconcilable with the nature of the claimants' attachment to those lands. This inherent limit arises because the relationship of an aboriginal community with its land should not be prevented from continuing into the future. Occupancy is determined by reference to the activities that have taken place on the land and the uses to which the land has been put by the particular group. If lands are so occupied, there will exist a special bond between the group and the land in question such that the land will be part of the definition of the group's distinctive culture. Land held by virtue of aboriginal title may not be alienated because the land has an inherent and unique value in itself, which is enjoyed by the community with aboriginal title to it. The community cannot put the land to uses which would destroy that value. Finally, the importance of the continuity of the relationship between an aboriginal community and its land, and the non-economic or inherent value of that land, should not be taken to detract from the possibility of surrender to the Crown in exchange for valuable consideration. On the contrary, the idea of surrender reinforces the conclusion that aboriginal title is limited. If aboriginal peoples wish to use their lands in a way that aboriginal title does not permit, then they must surrender those lands and convert them into non-title lands to do so.

Aboriginal title at common law was recognized well before 1982 and is accordingly protected in its full form by s. 35(1). The constitutionalization of common law aboriginal rights, however, does not mean that those rights exhaust the content of s. 35(1). The existence of an aboriginal right at common law is sufficient, but not necessary, for the recognition and affirmation of that right by s. 35(1).

Constitutionally recognized aboriginal rights fall along a spectrum with respect to their degree of connection with the land. At the one end are those aboriginal rights which are practices, customs and traditions integral to the distinctive aboriginal culture of the group claiming the right but where the use and occupation of the land where the activity is taking place is not sufficient to support a claim of title to the land. In the middle are activities which, out of necessity, take place on land and indeed, might be intimately related to a particular piece of land. Although an aboriginal group may not be able to demonstrate title to the land, it may nevertheless have a site-specific right to engage in a particular activity. At the other end of the spectrum is aboriginal title itself which confers more than the right to engage in site-specific activities which are aspects of the practices, customs and traditions of distinctive aboriginal cultures. Site-specific rights can be made out even if title cannot. Because aboriginal rights can vary with respect to their degree of connection with the land, some aboriginal groups may be unable to make out a claim to title, but will nevertheless possess aboriginal rights that are recognized and affirmed by s. 35(1), including site-specific rights to engage in particular activities.

Aboriginal title is a right to the land itself. That land may be used, subject to the inherent limitations of aboriginal title, for a variety of activities, none of which need be individually protected as aboriginal rights under s. 35(1). Those activities are parasitic on the underlying title. Section 35(1), since its purpose is to reconcile the prior presence of aboriginal peoples with the assertion of Crown sovereignty, must recognize and affirm both aspects of that prior presence—first, the occupation of land, and second, the prior social organization and distinctive cultures of aboriginal peoples on that land.

The test for the identification of aboriginal rights to engage in particular activities and the test for the identification of aboriginal title, although broadly similar, are distinct in two ways. First, under the test for aboriginal title, the requirement that the land be integral to the distinctive culture of the claimants is subsumed by the requirement of occupancy. Second, whereas the time for the identification of aboriginal rights is the time of first contact, the time for the identification of aboriginal title is the time at which the Crown asserted sovereignty over the land.

In order to establish a claim to aboriginal title, the aboriginal group asserting the claim must establish that it occupied the lands in question at the time at which the Crown asserted sovereignty over the land subject to the title. In the context of aboriginal title, sovereignty is the appropriate time period to consider for several reasons. First, from a theoretical standpoint, aboriginal title arises out of prior occupation of the land by aboriginal peoples and out of the relationship between the common law and pre-existing systems of aboriginal law. Aboriginal title is a burden on the Crown's underlying title. The Crown, however, did not gain this title until it asserted sovereignty and it makes no sense to speak of a burden on the underlying title before that title existed. Aboriginal title crystallized at the time sovereignty was asserted. Second, aboriginal title does not raise the problem of distinguishing between distinctive, integral aboriginal practices, customs and traditions and those influenced or introduced by European contact. Under common law, the act of occupation or possession is sufficient to ground aboriginal title and it is not necessary to prove that the land was a distinctive or integral part of the aboriginal society before the arrival of Europeans. Finally, the date of sovereignty is more certain than the date of first contact.

Both the common law and the aboriginal perspective on land should be taken into account in establishing the proof of occupancy. At common law, the fact of physical occupation is proof of possession at law, which in turn will ground title to the land. Physical occupation may be established in a variety of ways, ranging from the construction of dwellings through cultivation and enclosure of fields to regular use of definite tracts of land for hunting, fishing or otherwise exploiting its resources. In considering whether occupation sufficient to ground title is established, the group's size, manner of life, material resources, and technological abilities, and the character of the lands claimed must be taken into account. Given the occupancy requirement, it was not necessary to include as part of the test for aboriginal title whether a group demonstrated a connection with the piece of land as being of central significance to its distinctive culture. Ultimately, the question of physical occupation is one of fact to be determined at trial. If present occupation is relied on as proof of occupation pre-sovereignty, there must be a continuity between present and pre-sovereignty occupation. Since conclusive evidence of pre-sovereignty occupation may be difficult, an aboriginal community may provide evidence of present occupation as proof of pre-sovereignty occupation in support of a claim to aboriginal title. An unbroken chain of continuity need not be established between present and prior occupation. The fact that the nature of occupation has changed would not ordinarily preclude a claim for aboriginal title, as long as a substantial connection between the people and the land is maintained. The only limitation on this principle might be that the land not be used in ways which are inconsistent with continued use by future generations of aboriginals.

At sovereignty, occupation must have been exclusive. This requirement flows from the definition of aboriginal title itself, which is defined in terms of the right to exclusive use and occupation of land. The test must take into account the context of the aboriginal society at the time of sovereignty. The requirement of exclusive occupancy and the possibility of joint title can be reconciled by recognizing that joint title can arise from shared exclusivity. As well, shared, non-exclusive aboriginal rights short of aboriginal title but tied to the land and permitting a number of uses can be established if exclusivity cannot be proved. The common law should develop to recognize aboriginal rights as they were recognized by either *de facto* practice or by aboriginal systems of governance.

Per La Forest and L'Heureux-Dubé JJ.: "Aboriginal title" is based on the continued occupation and use of the land as part of the aboriginal peoples' traditional way of life. This *sui generis* interest is not equated with fee simple ownership; nor can it be described with reference to traditional property law concepts. It is personal in that it is generally inalienable except to the Crown and, in dealing with this interest, the Crown is subject to a fiduciary obligation to treat the aboriginal peoples fairly. There is reluctance to define more precisely the right of aboriginal peoples to live on their lands as their forefathers had lived.

The approach to defining the aboriginal right of occupancy is highly contextual. A distinction must be made between (1) the recognition of a general right to occupy and possess ancestral lands and (2) the recognition of a discrete right to engage in an aboriginal activity in a particular area. The latter has been defined as the traditional use, by a tribe of Indians, that has continued from pre-contact times of a particular area for a particular purpose. By contrast, a general claim to occupy and possess vast tracts of territory is the right to use the land for a variety of activities related to the aboriginal society's habits and mode of life. As well, in defining the nature of "aboriginal title", reference need not be made to statutory provisions and regulations dealing with reserve lands.

In defining the nature of "aboriginal title", reference need not be made to statutory provisions and regulations dealing specifically with reserve lands. Though the interest of an Indian band in a reserve has been found to be derived from, and to be of the same nature as, the interest of an aboriginal society in its traditional tribal lands, it does not follow that specific statutory provisions governing reserve lands should automatically apply to traditional tribal lands.

The "key" factors for recognizing aboriginal rights under s. 35(1) are met in the present case. First, the nature of an aboriginal claim must be identified precisely with regard to particular practices, customs and traditions. When dealing with a claim of "aboriginal title", the court will focus on the occupation and use of the land as part of the aboriginal society's traditional way of life.

Second, an aboriginal society must specify the area that has been continuously used and occupied by identifying general boundaries. Exclusivity means that an aboriginal group must show that a claimed territory is indeed its ancestral territory and not the territory of an unconnected aboriginal society. It is possible that two or more aboriginal groups may have occupied the same territory and therefore a finding of joint occupancy would not be precluded.

Third, the aboriginal right of possession is based on the continued occupation and use of traditional tribal lands since the assertion of Crown sovereignty. However, the date of sovereignty may not be the only relevant time to consider. Continuity may still exist where the present occupation of one area is connected to the pre-sovereignty occupation of another area. Also, aboriginal peoples claiming a right of possession may provide evidence of present occupation as proof of prior occupation. Further, it is not necessary to establish an unbroken chain of continuity.

Fourth, if aboriginal peoples continue to occupy and use the land as part of their traditional way of life, the land is of central significance to them. Aboriginal occupancy refers not only to the presence of aboriginal peoples in villages or permanently settled areas but also to the use of adjacent lands and even remote territories used to pursue a traditional mode of life. Occupancy is part of aboriginal culture in a broad sense and is, therefore, absorbed in the notion of distinctiveness. The *Royal Proclamation, 1763* supports this approach to occupancy.

McLachlin J. was in substantial agreement.

Infringements of Aboriginal Title: The Test of Justification
Per Lamer C.J. and Cory, McLachlin and Major JJ.: Constitutionally recognized aboriginal rights are not absolute and may be infringed by the federal and provincial governments if the infringement (1) furthers a compelling and substantial legislative objective and (2) is consistent with the special fiduciary relationship between the Crown and the aboriginal peoples. The development of agriculture, forestry, mining and hydroelectric power, the general economic development of the interior of British Columbia, protection of the environment or endangered species, and the building of infrastructure and the settlement of foreign populations to support those aims, are objectives consistent with this purpose. Three aspects of aboriginal title are relevant to the second part of the test. First, the right to exclusive use and occupation of land is relevant to the degree of scrutiny of the infringing measure or action. Second, the right to choose to what uses land can be put, subject to the ultimate limit that those uses

cannot destroy the ability of the land to sustain future generations of aboriginal peoples, suggests that the fiduciary relationship between the Crown and aboriginal peoples may be satisfied by the involvement of aboriginal peoples in decisions taken with respect to their lands. There is always a duty of consultation and, in most cases, the duty will be significantly deeper than mere consultation. And third, lands held pursuant to aboriginal title have an inescapable economic component which suggests that compensation is relevant to the question of justification as well. Fair compensation will ordinarily be required when aboriginal title is infringed.

Per La Forest and L'Heureux-Dubé JJ.: Rights that are recognized and affirmed are not absolute. Government regulation can therefore infringe upon aboriginal rights if it meets the test of justification under s. 35(1). The approach is highly contextual.

The general economic development of the interior of British Columbia, through agriculture, mining, forestry and hydroelectric power, as well as the related building of infrastructure and settlement of foreign populations, are valid legislative objectives that, in principle, satisfy the first part of the justification analysis. Under the second part, these legislative objectives are subject to accommodation of the aboriginal peoples' interests. This accommodation must always be in accordance with the honour and good faith of the Crown. One aspect of accommodation of "aboriginal title" entails notifying and consulting aboriginal peoples with respect to the development of the affected territory. Another aspect is fair compensation.

McLachlin J. was in substantial agreement.

Self-Government

Per The Court: The errors of fact made by the trial judge, and the resultant need for a new trial, made it impossible for this Court to determine whether the claim to self-government had been made out.

Extinguishment

Per Lamer C.J. and Cory, McLachlin and Major JJ.: Section 91(24) of the *Constitution Act, 1867* (the federal power to legislate in respect of Indians) carries with it the jurisdiction to legislate in relation to aboriginal title, and by implication, the jurisdiction to extinguish it. The ownership by the provincial Crown (under s. 109) of lands held pursuant to aboriginal title is separate from jurisdiction over those lands. Notwithstanding s. 91(24), provincial laws of general application apply *proprio vigore* to Indians and Indian lands.

A provincial law of general application cannot extinguish aboriginal rights. First, a law of general application cannot, by definition, meet the standard "of clear and plain intention" needed to extinguish aboriginal rights without being *ultra vires* the province. Second, s. 91(24) protects a core of federal jurisdiction even from provincial laws of general application through the operation of the doctrine of interjurisdictional immunity. That core has been described as matters touching on "Indianness" or the "core of Indianness".

Provincial laws which would otherwise not apply to Indians *proprio vigore* are allowed to do so by s. 88 of the *Indian Act* which incorporates by reference provincial laws of general application. This provision, however, does not "invigorate" provincial laws which are invalid because they are in relation to Indians and Indian lands.

Per La Forest and L'Heureux-Dubé JJ.: The province had no authority to extinguish aboriginal rights either under the *Constitution Act, 1867* or by virtue of s. 88 of the *Indian Act*.

McLachlin J. was in substantial agreement.

Cases Cited

By Lamer C.J.

Considered: *R. v. Sparrow*, [1990] 1 S.C.R. 1075; *R. v. Van der Peet*, [1996] 2 S.C.R. 507; *R. v. N.T.C. Smokehouse Ltd.*, [1996] 2 S.C.R. 672; *R. v. Gladstone*, [1996] 2 S.C.R. 723; *R. v. Adams*, [1996] 3 S.C.R. 101; *R. v. Côté*, [1996] 3 S.C.R. 139; *St. Catherine's Milling and Lumber Co. v. The Queen* (1888), 14 A.C. 46, aff'g *sub nom. St. Catharines Milling and Lumber Co. v. The Queen* (1887), 13 S.C.R. 577; *Calder v. Attorney-General of British Columbia*, [1973] S.C.R. 313; *Baker Lake v. Minister of Indian Affairs and Northern*

Development, [1980] 1 F.C. 518; *Guerin v. The Queen*, [1984] 2
S.C.R. 335; referred to: *R. v. Pamajewon*, [1996] 2 S.C.R. 821; *R.
v. Sioui*, [1990] 1 S.C.R. 1025; *Mabo v. Queensland* (1992), 107
A.L.R. 1; *Four B Manufacturing Ltd. v. United Garment Workers of
America*, [1980] 1 S.C.R. 1031; *Natural Parents v. Superintendent of
Child Welfare*, [1976] 2 S.C.R. 751; *Dick v. The Queen*, [1985] 2
S.C.R. 309; *Stein v. The Ship "Kathy K"*, [1976] 2 S.C.R. 802; *N.V.
Bocimar S.A. v. Century Insurance Co. of Canada*, [1987] 1 S.C.R.
1247; *Schwartz v. Canada*, [1996] 1 S.C.R. 254; *Chartier v. Attorney
General of Quebec*, [1979] 2 S.C.R. 474; *Kruger v. The Queen*, [1978]
1 S.C.R. 104; *R. v. Taylor* (1981), 62 C.C.C. (2d) 227; *Simon v. The
Queen*, [1985] 2 S.C.R. 387; *Uukw v. R.*, [1987] 6 W.W.R. 155;
Canadian Pacific Ltd. v. Paul, [1988] 2 S.C.R. 654; *Roberts v.
Canada*, [1989] 1 S.C.R. 322; *Blueberry River Indian Band v.
Canada (Department of Indian Affairs and Northern Development)*,
[1995] 4 S.C.R. 344; *Mitchell v. Peguis Indian Band*, [1990] 2
S.C.R. 85; *St. Mary's Indian Band v. Cranbrook (City)*, [1997] 2
S.C.R. 657; *United States v. Santa Fe Pacific Railroad Co.*, 314 U.S.
339 (1941); *R. v. Sutherland*, [1980] 2 S.C.R. 451; *R. v. Francis*,
[1988] 1 S.C.R. 1025; *Derrickson v. Derrickson*, [1986] 1 S.C.R. 285.

By La Forest J.

    Considered: *Calder v. Attorney-General of British Columbia*,
[1973] S.C.R. 313; *Guerin v. The Queen*, [1984] 2 S.C.R. 335; *Canadian Pacific Ltd. v. Paul*, [1988] 2 S.C.R. 654; *R. v. Van der Peet*,
[1996] 2 S.C.R. 507; *R. v. Côté*, [1996] 3 S.C.R. 139; *R. v. Gladstone*,
[1996] 2 S.C.R. 723; *R. v. N.T.C. Smokehouse Ltd.*, [1996] 2 S.C.R.
672; *R. v. Sparrow*, [1990] 1 S.C.R. 1075; referred to: *R. v. Wesley*,
[1932] 4 D.L.R. 774; *Sikyea v. The Queen*, [1964] S.C.R. 642, aff'g
R. v. Sikyea (1964), 43 D.L.R. (2d) 150.

Statutes and Regulations Cited

Constitution Act, 1867, ss. 91(24), 109.
Constitution Act, 1982, s. 35(1).
Indian Act, R.S.C., 1985, c. I-5, ss. 18, 88.
Indian Oil and Gas Act, R.S.C., 1985, c. I-7, s. 6(2).
Royal Proclamation, 1763, R.S.C., 1985, App. II, No.1.

Treaty Between Her Majesty And The United States Of America, For The Settlement Of The Oregon Boundary (Oregon Boundary Treaty, 1846), TS 120.

Authors Cited

Burn, E. H. Cheshire and Burn's *Modern Law of Real Property*, 14th ed. London: Butterworths, 1988.

Canada. Royal Commission on Aboriginal Peoples. *Report of the Royal Commission on Aboriginal Peoples*, vols. 1 (*Looking Forward, Looking Back*) and 2 (*Restructuring the Relationship*). Ottawa: The Commission, 1996.

Gagne, Jocelyn. "The Content of Aboriginal Title at Common Law: A Look at the Nishga Claim" (1982–83), 47 *Sask. L. Rev.* 309.

Hogg, Peter W. *Constitutional Law of Canada*, 3rd ed. Scarborough, Ont.: Carswell, 1992.

Howard, Michael Newman, Peter Crane and Daniel A. Hochberg. *Phipson on Evidence*, 14th ed. London: Sweet & Maxwell, 1990.

Macklem, Patrick. "First Nations Self-Government and the Borders of the Canadian Legal Imagination" (1991), 36 *McGill L.J.* 382.

McLeod, Clay. "The Oral Histories of Canada's Northern People, Anglo-Canadian Evidence Law, and Canada's Fiduciary Duty to First Nations: Breaking Down the Barriers of the Past" (1992), 30 *Alta. L. Rev.* 1276.

McNeil, Kent. *Common Law Aboriginal Title*. Oxford: Clarendon Press, 1989.

McNeil, Kent. "The Constitutional Rights of the Aboriginal Peoples of Canada" (1982), 4 *Sup. Ct. L. Rev.* 255.

McNeil, Kent. "The Meaning of Aboriginal Title". In Michael Asch, ed., *Aboriginal and Treaty Rights in Canada*. Vancouver: U.B.C. Press, 1997.

Megarry, Robert E., and H. W. R. Wade. *The Law of Real Property*, 4th ed. London: Stevens, 1975.

O'Reilly, James. "La *Loi constitutionnelle de 1982*, droit des autochtones" (1984), 25 *C. de D.* 125.

Pentney, William. "The Rights of the Aboriginal Peoples of Canada in the *Constitution Act, 1982* Part II—Section 35: The Substantive Guarantee" (1988), 22 *U.B.C. L. Rev.* 207.

Sanders, Douglas. "Pre-Existing Rights: The Aboriginal Peoples of Canada". In Gérald-A. Beaudoin and Ed Ratushny, eds., *The Canadian Charter of Rights and Freedoms*, 2nd ed. Toronto: Carswell, 1989, 707.

Sanders, Douglas. "The Rights of the Aboriginal Peoples of Canada" (1983), 61 *Can. Bar Rev.* 314.

Slattery, Brian. *Ancestral Lands, Alien Laws: Judicial Perspectives on Aboriginal Title*. Saskatoon: University of Saskatchewan Native Law Centre, 1983.

Slattery, Brian. "The Constitutional Guarantee of Aboriginal and Treaty Rights" (1982-83), 8 *Queen's L.J.* 232.

Slattery, Brian. "Understanding Aboriginal Rights" (1987), 66 *Can. Bar Rev.* 727.

APPEAL and CROSS-APPEAL from a judgment of the British Columbia Court of Appeal (1993), 30 B.C.A.C. 1, 49 W.A.C. 1, 104 D.L.R. (4th) 470, [1993] 5 W.W.R. 97, [1993] 5 C.N.L.R. 1, [1993] B.C.J. No. 1395 (QL), varying an order of McEachern C.J., [1991] 3 W.W.R. 97, [1991] 5 C.N.L.R. xiii, (1991), 79 D.L.R. (4th) 185, [1991] B.C.J. No. 525 (QL), and dismissing British Columbia's cross-appeal as abandoned. Appeal allowed in part; cross-appeal dismissed.

Stuart Rush, Q.C., *Peter Grant, Michael Jackson, Louise Mandell* and *David Paterson*, for the appellants and respondents on the cross-appeal, the Gitksan Hereditary Chiefs *et al.*

Marvin R. V. Storrow, Q.C., *Joanne R. Lysyk* and *Joseph C. McArthur*, for the appellants and respondents on the cross-appeal, the Wet'suwet'en Hereditary Chiefs *et al.*

Joseph J. Arvay, Q.C., *Mark G. Underhill* and *Brenda Edwards*, for the respondent and appellant on the cross-appeal, Her Majesty the Queen in Right of the Province of British Columbia.

Graham Garton, Q.C., *Judith Bowers, Q.C.*, *Murray T. Wolf* and *Geoffrey S. Lester*, for the respondent the Attorney General of Canada.

Arthur Pape, Harry A. Slade, Peter Hogg and *Jean Teillet*, for the intervener the First Nations Summit.

Jack Woodward and *Albert C. Peeling*, for the intervener the Westbank First Nation.

Marvin R. V. Storrow, Q.C., Joanne R. Lysyk and *Joseph C. McArthur*, for the interveners the Musqueam Nation *et al.*

J. Keith Lowes, for the interveners the B.C. Cattlemen's Association *et al.*

Charles F. Willms, for the intervener Skeena Cellulose Inc.

J. Edward Gouge, Q.C., and *Jill M. Marks*, for the intervener Alcan Aluminum Ltd.

The judgment of Lamer C.J. and Cory and Major JJ. was delivered by

THE CHIEF JUSTICE—

I. Introduction

1 This appeal is the latest in a series of cases in which it has fallen to this Court to interpret and apply the guarantee of existing aboriginal rights found in s. 35(1) of the *Constitution Act, 1982.* Although that line of decisions, commencing with *R. v. Sparrow,* [1990] 1 S.C.R. 1075, proceeding through the *Van der Peet* trilogy (*R. v. Van der Peet*, [1996] 2 S.C.R. 507, *R. v. N.T.C. Smokehouse Ltd.*, [1996] 2 S.C.R. 672, and *R. v. Gladstone*, [1996] 2 S.C.R. 723), and ending in *R. v. Pamajewon*, [1996] 2 S.C.R. 821, *R. v. Adams*, [1996] 3 S.C.R. 101, and *R. v. Côté*, [1996] 3 S.C.R. 139, have laid down the jurisprudential framework for s. 35(1), this appeal raises a set of interrelated and novel questions which revolve around a single issue—the nature and scope of the constitutional protection afforded by s. 35(1) to common law aboriginal title.

2 In *Adams*, and in the companion decision in *Côté*, I considered and rejected the proposition that claims to aboriginal rights must also be grounded in an underlying claim to aboriginal title. But I held, nevertheless, that aboriginal title was a distinct species of aboriginal right that was recognized and affirmed by s. 35(1). Since aboriginal title was not being claimed in those earlier appeals, it was unnecessary to say more. This appeal demands,

however, that the Court now explore and elucidate the implications of the constitutionalization of aboriginal title. The first is the specific content of aboriginal title, a question which this Court has not yet definitively addressed, either at common law or under s. 35(1). The second is the related question of the test for the proof of title, which, whatever its content, is a right *in land*, and its relationship to the definition of the aboriginal rights recognized and affirmed by s. 35(1) in *Van der Peet* in terms of *activities*. The third is whether aboriginal title, as a right in land, mandates a modified approach to the test of justification first laid down in *Sparrow* and elaborated upon in *Gladstone*.

3 In addition to the relationship between aboriginal title and s. 35(1), this appeal also raises an important practical problem relevant to the proof of aboriginal title which is endemic to aboriginal rights litigation generally—the treatment of the oral histories of Canada's aboriginal peoples by the courts. In *Van der Peet*, I held that the common law rules of evidence should be adapted to take into account the *sui generis* nature of aboriginal rights. In this appeal, the Court must address what specific form those modifications must take.

4 Finally, given the existence of aboriginal title in British Columbia, this Court must address, on cross-appeal, the question of whether the province of British Columbia, from the time it joined Confederation in 1871, until the entrenchment of s. 35(1) in 1982, had jurisdiction to extinguish the rights of aboriginal peoples, including aboriginal title, in that province. Moreover, if the province was without this jurisdiction, a further question arises—whether provincial laws of general application that would otherwise be inapplicable to Indians and Indian lands could nevertheless extinguish aboriginal rights through the operation of s. 88 of the *Indian Act*, R.S.C., 1985, c. I-5.

II. Facts

5 At the British Columbia Supreme Court, McEachern C.J. heard 374 days of evidence and argument. Some of that evidence was not in a form which is familiar to common law courts, including oral histories and legends. Another significant part was the

evidence of experts in genealogy, linguistics, archeology, anthropology, and geography.

6 The trial judge's decision (reported at [1991] 3 W.W.R. 97) is nearly 400 pages long, with another 100 pages of schedules. Although I am of the view that there must be a new trial, I nevertheless find it useful to summarize some of the relevant facts, so as to put the remainder of the judgment into context.

A. *The Claim at Trial*

7 This action was commenced by the appellants, who are all Gitksan or Wet'suwet'en hereditary chiefs, who, both individually and on behalf of their "Houses" claimed separate portions of 58,000 square kilometres in British Columbia. For the purpose of the claim, this area was divided into 133 individual territories, claimed by the 71 Houses. This represents all of the Wet'suwet'en people, and all but 12 of the Gitksan Houses. Their claim was originally for "ownership" of the territory and "jurisdiction" over it. (At this Court, this was transformed into, primarily, a claim for aboriginal title over the land in question.) The province of British Columbia counterclaimed for a declaration that the appellants have no right or interest in and to the territory or alternatively, that the appellants' cause of action ought to be for compensation from the Government of Canada.

B. *The Gitksan and Wet'suwet'en Peoples*

(1) *Demography*

8 The Gitksan consist of approximately 4,000 to 5,000 persons, most of whom now live in the territory claimed, which is generally the watersheds of the north and central Skeena, Nass and Babine Rivers and their tributaries. The Wet'suwet'en consist of approximately 1,500 to 2,000 persons, who also predominantly live in the territory claimed. This territory is mainly in the watersheds of the Bulkley and parts of the Fraser-Nechako River systems and their tributaries. It lies immediately east and south of the Gitksan.

9 Of course, the Gitksan and Wet'suwet'en are not the only people living in the claimed territory. As noted by both McEachern C.J. at trial (at p. 440) and Lambert J.A. on appeal (at p. 243),

there are other aboriginals who live in the claimed territory, notably the Carrier-Sekani and Nishga peoples. Some of these people have unsettled land claims overlapping with the territory at issue here. Moreover, there are also numerous non-aboriginals living there. McEachern C.J. found that, at the time of the trial, the non-aboriginal population in the territory was over 30,000.

(2) *History*

10   There were numerous theories of the history of the Gitksan and Wet'suwet'en peoples before the trial judge. His conclusion from the evidence was that their ancestors migrated from Asia, probably through Alaska, and spread south and west into the areas which they found to be liveable. There was archeological evidence, which he accepted, that there was some form of human habitation in the territory and its surrounding areas from 3,500 to 6,000 years ago, and intense occupation of the Hagwilget Canyon site (near Hazelton), prior to about 4,000 to 3,500 years ago. This occupation was mainly in or near villages on the Skeena River, the Babine River or the Bulkley River, where salmon, the staple of their diet, was easily obtainable. The other parts of the territory surrounding and between their villages and rivers were used for hunting and gathering for both food and ceremonial purposes. The scope of this hunting and gathering area depended largely on the availability of the required materials in the areas around the villages. Prior to the commencement of the fur trade, there was no reason to travel far from the villages for anything other than their subsistence requirements.

(3) *North American Exploration*

11   There was little European influence in western Canada until the arrival of Capt. Cook at Nootka on Vancouver Island in 1778, which led to the sea otter hunt in the north Pacific. This influence grew with the establishment of the first Hudson's Bay trading post west of the Rockies (although east of the territories claimed) by Simon Fraser in 1805–1806. Trapping for the commercial fur trade was not an aboriginal practice, but rather one influenced by European contact. The trial judge held that the time of direct contact

between the Aboriginal Peoples in the claimed territory was approximately 1820, after the trader William Brown arrived and Hudson's Bay had merged with the North West Company.

(4) *Present Social Organization*

12 McEachern C.J. set out a description of the present social organization of the appellants. In his opinion, this was necessary because "one of the ingredients of aboriginal land claims is that they arise from long-term communal rather than personal use or possession of land" (at p. 147). The fundamental premise of both the Gitksan and the Wet'suwet'en peoples is that they are divided into clans and Houses. Every person born of a Gitksan or Wet'suwet'en woman is automatically a member of his or her mother's House and clan. There are four Gitksan and four Wet'-suwet'en clans, which are subdivided into Houses. Each House has one or more Hereditary Chief as its titular head, selected by the elders of their House, as well as possibly the Head Chief of the other Houses of the clan. There is no head chief for the clans, but there is a ranking order of precedence within communities or villages, where one House or clan may be more prominent than others.

13 At trial, the appellants' claim was based on their historical use and "ownership" of one or more of the territories. The trial judge held that these are marked, in some cases, by physical and tangible indicators of their association with the territories. He cited as examples totem poles with the Houses' crests carved, or distinctive regalia. In addition, the Gitksan Houses have an "adaawk" which is a collection of sacred oral tradition about their ancestors, histories and territories. The Wet'suwet'en each have a "kungax" which is a spiritual song or dance or performance which ties them to their land. Both of these were entered as evidence on behalf of the appellants (see my discussion of the trial judge's view of this evidence, *infra*).

14 The most significant evidence of spiritual connection between the Houses and their territory is a feast hall. This is where the Gitksan and Wet'suwet'en peoples tell and retell their stories and identify their territories to remind themselves of the sacred

connection that they have with their lands. The feast has a ceremonial purpose, but is also used for making important decisions.
The trial judge also noted the *Criminal Code* prohibition on aboriginal feast ceremonies, which existed until 1951.

III. Judgments Below
A. *Supreme Court of British Columbia*
(1) *General Principles*

15 The trial judge began his analysis by considering the signi-
ficant cases in this area: *St. Catharines Milling and Lumber Co. v.
The Queen* (1887), 13 S.C.R. 577, *Calder v. Attorney-General of
British Columbia*, [1973] S.C.R. 313, *Baker Lake v. Minister of
Indian Affairs and Northern Development*, [1980] 1 F.C. 518 (T.D.),
Guerin v. The Queen, [1984] 2 S.C.R. 335, *R. v. Sioui*, [1990] 1
S.C.R. 1025, and *Sparrow, supra*. On the basis of this jurisprudence, he set out four propositions of law. First, aboriginal interests arise out of occupation or use of specific land for aboriginal
purposes for an indefinite or long, long time before the assertion
of sovereignty. Second, aboriginal interests are communal, consisting of subsistence activities and are not proprietary. Third, at common law, aboriginal rights exist at the pleasure of the Crown and
may be extinguished when the intention of the Crown is clear and
plain. This power reposed with the Imperial Crown during the
colonial period. Upon Confederation the province obtained title
to all Crown land in the province subject to the "interests" of the
Indians. Finally, unextinguished aboriginal rights are not absolute. Crown action and aboriginal rights may, in proper circumstances, be reconciled. Generally speaking, aboriginal rights may
be regulated by the Crown only when such regulation operates to
interfere with aboriginal rights pursuant to legitimate Crown
objectives which can honourably be justified, without undue
interference with such rights. Moreover, when regulating, government must be mindful of the appropriate level of priority which
aboriginal rights have over competing, inconsistent activities.

16 With respect to the appellants' claims, McEachern C.J.
divided his analysis into three parts: (1) jurisdiction over the territory; (2) ownership of the territory; and (in the alternative)

(3) particular aboriginal rights over the territory. In the ownership claim, the appellants asserted they were "absolutely entitled to occupy and possess the individual territories" claimed (at p. 126). The claim to jurisdiction was understood by the trial judge as comprising jurisdiction over land and people in the territory, and amounted to aboriginal sovereignty, a right to "govern the territory free of provincial control in all matters where their aboriginal laws conflict with the general law" (at p. 128). Although the claim advanced at trial was advanced by individual chiefs on behalf of themselves or their House members, the trial judge held that since aboriginal rights are communal in nature, any judgment must be for the benefit of the Gitksan and Wet'suwet'en peoples generally.

(2) *Aboriginal Ownership*

17 McEachern C.J. started from the proposition, for which he cited *St. Catharines Milling*, that aboriginal rights are not proprietary in nature, but rather "personal and usufructuary", and dependent upon the good will of the Sovereign. He was satisfied that at the date of British sovereignty, the appellants' ancestors were living in their villages on the great rivers, in a form of communal society. He was satisfied that they were occupying or possessing fishing sites and the adjacent lands, as their ancestors had done for the purpose of hunting and gathering that which they required for sustenance. However, he was not satisfied that they owned the territory in its entirety in any sense that would be recognized by the law.

18 There were several specific claims of the plaintiffs as to their uses of the land before the assertion of sovereignty. He concluded that the appellants' ancestors lived within the territory, but predominantly at the village sites. He accepted, at p. 372, that they harvested the resources of the lands, but that there was only evidence of "commonsense subsistence practices … entirely compatible with bare occupation for the purposes of subsistence". He was not persuaded that there was any system of governance or uniform custom relating to land outside the villages. He refused to accept that the spiritual beliefs exercised within the territory were necessarily common to all the people or that they were

universal practices. He was not persuaded that the present institutions of the plaintiffs' society were recognized by their ancestors.
Rather, he found, at p. 373, that "they more likely acted as they did
because of survival instincts". He stated that the maintenance and
protection of the boundaries were unproven because of the
numerous intrusions into the territory by other peoples. The oral
histories, totem poles and crests were not sufficiently reliable or
site specific to discharge the plaintiff's burden of proof. Although
McEachern C.J. recognized the social importance of the feast system and the fact that it evolved from earlier practices, he did not
accept its role in the management and allocation of lands, particularly after the fur trade. McEachern C.J. concluded, at p. 383,
that "I cannot infer from the evidence that the Indians possessed
or controlled any part of the territory, other than for village sites
and for aboriginal use in a way that would justify a declaration
equivalent to ownership".

19 Although he was of the opinion that the status of the villages and their immediate surrounding area may be different from
the territory as a whole, they were already predominantly reserve
lands. Hence, the question of the Gitksan and Wet'suwet'en
peoples' rights to these particular lands did not need to be dealt
with. Moreover, to the extent that there were hunting grounds not
included on those lands, McEachern C.J. believed he had no
jurisdiction to extend their boundaries.

(3) Aboriginal Sovereignty

20 McEachern C.J. interpreted the appellants' claim for "jurisdiction" as a claim to govern the territories in question. This
would include the right to enforce existing aboriginal law, as well
as make and enforce new laws, as required for the governance of
the people and their land. Most notably, this would also include a
right to supersede the laws of British Columbia if the two were in
conflict. McEachern C.J. rejected the appellants' claim for a right
of self-government, relying on both the sovereignty of the Crown
at common law, and what he considered to be the relative paucity
of evidence regarding an established governance structure. First,
he stated, at p. 386, that when British Columbia was united with

Canada, "all legislative jurisdiction was divided between Canada and the province, and there was no room for aboriginal jurisdiction or sovereignty which would be recognized by the law or the courts". Second, he characterized the Gitksan and Wet'suwet'en legal system, at p. 379, as a "most uncertain and highly flexible set of customs which are frequently not followed by the Indians themselves". He continued, at pp. 379–80, stating:

> I heard many instances of prominent Chiefs conducting themselves other than in accordance with these rules, such as logging or trapping on another chief's territory, although there always seemed to be an aboriginal exception which made almost any departure from aboriginal rules permissible. In my judgment, these rules are so flexible and uncertain that they cannot be classified as laws.

As a result of the flexibility and uncertainty of the customs and rules, McEachern C.J. rejected the appellants' claim to jurisdiction or sovereignty over the territories.

(4) *Aboriginal Rights*
21 After rejecting the appellants' claim for ownership of and jurisdiction over the disputed territories, McEachern C.J. turned to the possibility that the appellants nevertheless have aboriginal rights exercisable therein. He set out, at p. 388, the four part test from *Baker Lake* for an aboriginal right:

1. That they (the plaintiffs) and their ancestors were members of an organized society.
2. That the organized society occupied the specific territory over which they assert the aboriginal title.
3. That the occupation was to the exclusion of other organized societies.
4. That the occupation was an established fact at the time sovereignty was asserted by England.

McEachern C.J. noted that the requirement for an organized society had been satisfied, even though he did not believe the appellants' ancestors had institutions and governed themselves. However, he held that no specific level of sophistication ought to be required in satisfying this requirement. He then stated that there was evidence that the ancestors of the plaintiffs occupied specific locations in the territory (the villages) and they used surrounding lands. Although there was evidence that the Gitksan and Wet'suwet'en would not have been able to keep invaders or traders out of their territory, no other organized societies had established themselves in the core areas on any permanent basis. Moreover, he noted at the outset of his reasons on this point that he was uncertain about the requirement for exclusivity.

22 The activities that were to be protected were only those carried on at the time of contact or European influence and that were still carried on at the time of sovereignty. This included "all those sustenance practices and the gathering of all those products of the land and waters of the territory I shall define which they practised and used before exposure to European civilization (or sovereignty) for subsistence or survival" (at p. 391). This did not include trapping for the fur trade, or other land-based commercial enterprise. McEachern C.J. ultimately concluded, at p. 395 that "the plaintiffs have established, as of the date of British sovereignty, the requirements for continued residence in their villages, and for non-exclusive aboriginal sustenance rights within [certain] portions of the territory".

(5) Extinguishment and Fiduciary Duties

23 McEachern C.J. started with the proposition, at pp. 396–97, that the law "never recognized that the settlement of new lands depended upon the consent of the Indians". All aboriginal rights existed at the pleasure of the Crown, and could be extinguished by unilateral act. He accepted the "clear and plain" intention test for extinguishment, but took the view that it need not be express or even mention aboriginal rights, if the intention can be identified by necessary implication. An example of such implied extinguishment might be a fee simple grant to a third party, or a grant of a lease, licence, permit or other tenure inconsistent with continuing aboriginal interest.

24 McEachern C.J. held that any aboriginal rights to the land had been extinguished. The extinguishment arose out of certain colonial enactments which demonstrated an intention to manage Crown lands in a way that was inconsistent with continuing aboriginal rights. He stated, at p. 411, that "the Crown with full knowledge of the local situation fully intended to settle the colony and to grant titles and tenures unburdened by any aboriginal interests". Crown grantees who received land in colonial times were clearly intended to receive the land free from any aboriginal encumbrances. Moreover, this intention to extinguish did not only apply to lands that had actually been granted to third parties, but rather all Crown land in British Columbia. However, it should be noted that he was careful to distinguish between land and fishing rights. Since McEachern C.J. was of the view that all aboriginal title to the territories in question had been extinguished during colonial times, it was not necessary to consider whether the province had the power to extinguish aboriginal rights after Confederation.

25 Notwithstanding the complete extinguishment of all aboriginal rights in land, McEachern C.J. held, at p. 417, that the Crown was under a fiduciary obligation to continue to allow native persons to use vacant crown lands for lawful purposes until the land "is dedicated to another purpose". This is not an aboriginal "right", to which s. 35 can be applied, since any such "rights" over the land had been extinguished. However, he held that where the Crown extinguishes an aboriginal right, and makes a promise regarding use of Crown land at the same time, this creates the same fiduciary obligation as if the aboriginal people had surrendered the land to the Crown. In articulating guidelines for the application of the Crown's fiduciary obligation, McEachern C.J. made it clear that the Crown must be free to direct resource management in the province in the best interests of both the aboriginal and non-aboriginal persons in the province. However, Crown authorities should always keep the "aboriginal interests of the plaintiffs very much in mind" (at p. 423) in developing policies for the territory, and should ensure that aboriginal activities on the land are not unduly impaired.

(6) *Damages*

26 Since the plaintiffs failed to establish that existing owner-ship, jurisdiction, or aboriginal rights had been breached, the claim for damages for wrongful appropriation of their territory was dismissed by McEachern C.J.

(7) *Lands Subject to Aboriginal Rights at Sovereignty*

27 McEachern C.J. felt it necessary to delineate the boundaries of the lands that were subject to aboriginal rights at the time of sovereignty in case he was wrong that these rights had been extin-guished. He considered the evidence regarding the external boundary of the territory, and the internal boundaries therein. He found numerous inconsistencies, and generally did not find it to be reliable. He rejected the boundaries as put forth by the appellants.

28 Nevertheless, since he had held that the Gitksan and Wet'-suwet'en had aboriginal sustenance rights over part of the land, he had to delineate their boundaries. He put forth three alternatives, and ultimately chose "Map 5" (at p. 400). This area recognized that the plaintiffs' ancestors likely used more distant areas in the territory. However, McEachern C.J. was not persuaded of such use in either the northernmost or southernmost portions of the territory. The northern boundary was drawn through the centre of the Skeena River, with 20 miles on the north side of the river being added. The southern boundary was drawn following some of the internal boundaries, but excluding several of the southern Wet'suwet'en individual territories. He selected this alternative because it worked less injustice for the Wet'suwet'en who lived more spread out and less concentrated near the rivers. However, he cut off the north and south portions of the claimed territory because he did not have confidence in the presence of the Gitk-san or Wet'suwet'en in the areas north or south of the boundaries he drew.

(8) *Other Matters*

29 McEachern C.J. concluded his reasons by rejecting the province's argument that the plaintiffs' aboriginal rights to some of the lands had been abandoned. He did not think courts should

be quick to treat aboriginal lands as abandoned. He could not say with confidence which lands should be abandoned, and which should not, even though there was clearly declining aboriginal use of some of the lands. He also stressed that the onus of demonstrating abandonment rested with the province and that they had not discharged that onus. He also rejected the argument that the plaintiffs had waived their rights by accepting and using reserves and by conforming to the general law of the province. The honour of the Crown precluded the province from relying on this defence.

(9) *Final Order*

30 In result, therefore, McEachern C.J. dismissed the action against Canada, dismissed the plaintiffs' claims for ownership and jurisdiction and for aboriginal rights in the territory, granted a declaration that the plaintiffs were entitled to use unoccupied or vacant land subject to the general law of the province, dismissed the claim for damages and dismissed the province's counterclaim. No order for costs was made.

B. *British Columbia Court of Appeal*
(1) *Judgment of Macfarlane J.A. (Taggart J.A. concurring)*

31 Macfarlane J.A. set out the following propositions of law which he indicated were the starting points for analysing aboriginal rights in land, which he garnered from *Baker Lake, Calder, Guerin, Sparrow*, and *Mabo v. Queensland* (1992), 107 A.L.R. 1 (H.C.). First, such rights arise from historic occupation and possession of the aboriginal peoples' tribal lands. Second, they arise by operation of law and do not depend on a grant from the Crown. Third, they are not absolute, but they are subject to regulation and extinguishment. Fourth, they are *sui generis* communal rights. Fifth, they cannot be alienated other than to the Crown. Finally, they are related to aboriginal activities which formed an integral part of traditional Indian life prior to sovereignty.

(a) Ownership Rights

32 Examining the appellants' ownership claim, Macfarlane J.A. agreed that an exclusive right to occupy land is required to

support a claim akin to ownership. He noted that the use of the term "ownership" (which was used in the plaintiffs in their pleadings) was unfortunate, since *Guerin* specifically held that the aboriginal interest does not amount to beneficial ownership. In his view, the trial judge properly applied the law to the plaintiffs' claim of ownership. Similarly, he found no merit in the appellants' challenge to the trial judge's findings of fact on a number of points. Although some of the areas of the evidence were cause for concern, he concluded that the issues required an interpretation of the evidence as a whole and that it would be inappropriate for this court to intervene and substitute its opinions for that of the trial judge. Hence, he did not disturb the judge's conclusion with regard to ownership of the territory, nor his conclusion that any interest which the appellants have in the land is not proprietary.

(b) Aboriginal Sustenance Rights

33 Macfarlane J.A. canvassed the trial judge's findings regarding aboriginal sustenance rights. He noted that McEachern C.J.'s error in requiring a "time-depth" of a long time prior to contact in order to establish the rights did not affect his view of the territorial limits of the right. He agreed with the trial judge's application of the *Baker Lake* test. In particular, he viewed the significant question to be whether the practices were integral to aboriginal society or had only resulted from European influences. Macfarlane J.A. concluded that it would be inappropriate to intervene and substitute his view for that of the trial judge with respect to the weight of the evidence. Hence, if the appellants succeeded on the appeal with respect to extinguishment, they were entitled to sustenance rights in the area as identified by McEachern C.J. on Map 5.

(c) Jurisdiction

34 Macfarlane J.A. essentially agreed with the trial judge with respect to his analysis of the jurisdiction, or sovereignty issue. He characterized the claim as the right to control and manage the use of lands and resources in the territory, as well as the right to govern the people within the territory, to the possible exclusion of

laws of general application within the province. He stated that the Gitksan and Wet'suwet'en peoples do not need a court declaration to permit internal self-regulation, if they consent to be governed. However, the rights of self-government encompassing a power to make general laws governing the land, resources, and people in the territory are legislative powers which cannot be awarded by the courts. Such jurisdiction is inconsistent with the *Constitution Act, 1867* and its division of powers. When the Crown imposed English law on all the inhabitants of the colony and when British Columbia entered Confederation, the aboriginal people became subject to Canadian (and provincial) legislative authority. For this reason, the claim to jurisdiction failed.

(d) Extinguishment

35 Macfarlane J.A. began by noting that treaty-making is the most desirable way to resolve aboriginal land issues. However, he noted that prior to 1982, the rights of aboriginal people could be extinguished by the unilateral act of the sovereign, without the consent of the aboriginal people. Intention to extinguish must be clear and plain. Although express language is not strictly necessary, the honour of the Crown requires its intentions to be either express or manifested by unavoidable implication. Unavoidable implication should not be easily found—it occurs only where the interpretation of the instrument permits no other result. This, in turn, depends on the nature of the aboriginal interest and of the impugned grant.

36 Macfarlane J.A. disagreed with the trial judge that the colonial instruments manifested the required clear and plain intention to extinguish all aboriginal interests in land. The purpose of the colonial instruments in question was to facilitate an orderly settlement of the province, and to give the Crown control over grants to third parties. It is not inevitable, upon a reading of the statutory scheme, that the aboriginal interest was to be disregarded. They did not foreclose the possibility of treaties or of co-existence of aboriginal and Crown interests. Similarly, even fee simple grants to third parties do not necessarily exclude aboriginal use. For example, uncultivated vacant land held in fee simple does not

necessarily preclude the exercise of hunting rights. Moreover, it is clear that, at common law, two or more interests in land less than fee simple can co-exist. However, since the record was not sufficiently specific to permit the detailed analysis of such issues, Macfarlane J.A. suggested that these issues be dealt with in negotiation. He concluded that extinguishment by a particular grant needed to be determined on a case by case basis.

37   Macfarlane J.A. considered the constitutional power of the province to extinguish aboriginal rights after 1871, and in particular, whether valid provincial legislation could extinguish aboriginal rights in land by incidental effect. After 1871, the exclusive power to legislate in relation to "Indians, and Lands reserved for the Indians" was given to the federal government by virtue of s. 91(24) of the *Constitution Act, 1867*. Valid provincial legislation may apply to Indians, so long as it is a law of general application and not one that affects their Indianness, their status, or their core values (*Four B Manufacturing Ltd. v. United Garment Workers of America*, [1980] 1 S.C.R. 1031; *Natural Parents v. Superintendent of Child Welfare*, [1976] 2 S.C.R. 751; *Dick v. The Queen*, [1985] 2 S.C.R. 309). However, the proposition that provincial laws could extinguish Indian title by incidental effect must be examined in light of federal authority relating to Indians and of the aboriginal perspective. The traditional homelands of aboriginal people are integral to their traditional way of life and their self-concept. If the effect of provincial legislation were to strip the aboriginal people of the use and occupation of their traditional homelands, it would be an impermissible intrusion into federal jurisdiction, as such a law would "trench on the very core of the subject matter of s. 91(24)" (at p. 169). Hence, he concluded that provincial legislatures do not have the constitutional competence to extinguish common law aboriginal rights. Moreover, extinguishment by adverse dominion could only be accomplished by the federal government. Similarly, s. 88 of the *Indian Act* did not assist the province. Laws of general application which do not affect the "core of Indianness" apply by their own force. However, provincial laws which do affect that core rely on s. 88, which referentially incorporates them into federal law. For s. 88 of the

Indian Act to give the province authority to extinguish aboriginal rights, it would have to show a clear and plain intention to do so. Since no such intention exists in s. 88 in particular or the *Indian Act* in general, it cannot authorize outright extinguishment. However, it may authorize provincial regulation of and interference with aboriginal rights. Of course, now the operation of such regulations are now subject to s. 35 of the *Constitution Act, 1982*.

(e) Relief Allowed

38 Macfarlane J.A. granted a declaration that the plaintiffs' aboriginal rights were not all extinguished by the colonial instruments enacted prior to British Columbia's entry into Confederation in 1871. He also granted a declaration that the appellants have unextinguished, non-exclusive aboriginal rights, formerly protected at common law, and now protected under s. 35(1) of the *Constitution Act, 1982*. These rights are not ownership or property rights, and are located within the area indicated on Map 5. Their characteristics may vary depending on the particular context in which the rights are said to exist, and are dependent on the specific facts of each case.

39 Macfarlane J.A. did not grant a declaration with respect to jurisdiction over land and resources or people within the territory, leaving this to negotiation. He also did not interfere with the decision of the trial judge that the claim for damages must be dismissed. He noted that the parties wished to negotiate the precise location, scope, content and consequences of the aboriginal rights which the trial judge has held may be exercised in that part of the territory, the approximate area of which is illustrated on Map 5. However, no order of the court was required to permit the parties to enter into such negotiations.

40 Finally, Macfarlane J.A. stated that he would not give effect to the alternative declarations sought by the province relating to the alleged extinguishment of aboriginal rights by grants of fee simple and of lesser interests in the period from 1871–1982. The province did not have the power after 1871 to extinguish aboriginal rights. However, some provincial land and resource laws affecting aboriginal rights may be given force as federal laws through the

operation of s. 88 of the *Indian Act*. The effect of fee simple and lesser grants on the particular aboriginal rights would require a detailed and complete analysis, which neither the record nor the submissions permitted. He made no order for costs, adopting the reasons of the trial judge.

(2) *Wallace J.A. (concurring)*
(a) Scope of Appellate Review

41 Wallace J.A. considered the appropriate principles for appellate review of a trial judge's findings of fact. An appellate court should find error on the part of the trial judge with respect to those aspects of the finding of facts which involve questions of credibility or weight to be given the evidence of a witness only if it is established that the trial judge made some "palpable and overriding error" which affected his assessment of the material facts. Such an error exists in three situations: firstly, when it can be demonstrated there was no evidence to support a material finding of fact of the trial judge; secondly, when the trial judge wrongly overlooked admissible evidence relevant and material to the issue before the court; or thirdly, where the trial judge's finding of fact cannot be supported as reasonable. In reversing the trial judge for "palpable and overriding error" the Court of Appeal must designate the specific error and state why the nature of the error justifies reversing the trial judge's finding of fact. Wallace J.A. held that these principles applied to the trial judge's determination of the nature and territorial scope of the aboriginal activities, the question of jurisdiction and control over the territory, and the weight to be attributed to the evidence of the various witnesses.

(b) General Principles

42 Wallace J.A. stated that aboriginal rights of occupation and use originate in the Indians' historic occupation and use of their tribal lands, and is recognized by the common law. Unlike the trial judge, he recognized that these rights may resemble a proprietary title, not unlike those in western property law systems, or they may be restricted to certain uses of the land. He set out the requirements for establishing aboriginal rights, varying from the

Baker Lake test used by the trial judge. In Wallace J.A.'s formulation of the test, the practices supporting the rights in question had to be integral to the claimants' distinctive and traditional society or culture. Moreover, he resolved the trial judge's concerns about the requirement of exclusivity as follows: if the plaintiffs claim exclusive occupation and use, the traditional occupation had to be to the exclusion of other organized societies.

(c) Aboriginal Ownership

43 Wallace J.A. considered there to be reasonable support for the trial judge's conclusions regarding the nature and scope of the appellants' interest in the territory. The standard of occupation required to support the claim of ownership depended on the nature of the interest. The appellants' claim was to manage the lands and natural resources. This suggests exclusive control and possession of the territory, requiring the appellants to demonstrate exclusive possession. Since they could not do so, he concluded that the trial judge correctly dismissed their claim for ownership.

(d) Aboriginal Rights of Occupation and Use of Traditional Lands

44 Even if the appellants' claim were characterized as a claim for aboriginal title, rather than ownership, Wallace J.A. agreed with the criteria applied by the trial judge: the occupation of specific territory, the exclusion of other organized societies, occupation at the time of British sovereignty and long-time aboriginal practices. Applying these principles to the trial judge's findings of fact, Wallace J.A. concluded that the appellants had not established a manifest or palpable error in concluding that the appellants' rights were non-exclusive, and confined to user rights. However, he was of the view that the court was not in a position to express an opinion on the specific territorial scope of these rights.

(e) Aboriginal Jurisdiction or Self-Government

45 Wallace J.A. agreed that the claim for "jurisdiction" was for an undefined form of government over land and people in the

territory, which would be paramount as against provincial laws in the case of a conflict. Wallace J.A. held, at p. 225, that this claim was "incompatible with every principle of the parliamentary sovereignty which vested in the Imperial Parliament in 1846". Moreover, British Columbia's entry into Canada in 1871 exhaustively distributed legislative power between the province and the federal government. Section 35 of the *Constitution Act, 1982* could not revive and protect any sovereignty rights which the Gitksan and Wet'suwet'en may have had.

(f) Extinguishment

46 Wallace J.A. agreed with Macfarlane J.A. on this issue. He set out the test ("clear and plain intention") and decided that the rights of use and occupation discussed above had not been extinguished.

(g) Miscellaneous

47 Wallace J.A. agreed that the appellants' damages claim should be dismissed, without deciding whether damages might be payable for wrongful interference with the Gitksan's and Wet'-suwet'en's non-exclusive aboriginal rights in the territory. He also considered the appellants' claim that the appeal be adjourned in part for two years, during which time the parties would attempt to negotiate an agreement regarding the geographic parameters of the claimed territory. The court would retain jurisdiction to determine issues or refer them to the trial court if the parties failed to reach an agreement during the two-year period. However, he noted that the role of the Court of Appeal is not to tailor its judgment to facilitate negotiation. The Court of Appeal is restricted to declaring the legal status of rights claimed, on the basis of the trial record.

(3) *Lambert J.A. (dissenting)*
(a) General Principles

48 Lambert J.A. considered at length the leading cases with regard to aboriginal rights in British Columbia. He set out a number of conclusions. He recognized that aboriginal title and

aboriginal rights are *sui generis*, and not easily explicable in terms of ordinary western jurisprudential analysis or common law concepts. He noted that aboriginal title is a form of aboriginal rights, and is therefore protected by s. 35. All rights arise from the practices, customs and traditions which form an integral part of the distinctive culture of the aboriginal people, and were part of the social fabric of aboriginal society at the time of the arrival of the first Europeans. This co-existed with the settlers' common law rights from the time of contact until sovereignty. After that time, aboriginal rights that continued as part of the social fabric of the aboriginal society were protected by both their own internal institutions and the common law.

49 Lambert J.A. believed that aboriginal rights were not frozen at the time of contact. Rather, they must be permitted to maintain contemporary relevance in relation to the needs of the holders of the rights as those needs change along with the changes in overall society. The rights may be individual, or they may be collective, depending on how they were and are treated by aboriginal people. Moreover, they do not come from aboriginal practice dating from time immemorial. Rather, they come, under the doctrine of continuity, from the practices, customs and traditions of the aboriginal people.

50 Aboriginal rights are neither abrogated by the fact that similar rights may be held by non-aboriginal people nor because the holders of the rights participate in the wage or cash economy. A right to occupy, possess, use and enjoy land to the exclusion of all others does not mean that it must be confined to the activities carried on in 1846, or that its exercise requires a renunciation of the contemporary world.

(b) Extinguishment

51 Lambert J.A. considered the test for extinguishment from *Calder*, and expressly rejected Judson J.'s views. He derived the authority to do so from the way in which extinguishment was dealt with in *Sparrow*. In considering implicit extinguishment, he stated that it will only be held to occur where no other conclusion is possible from the particular instrument or conduct. It could not

take place through adverse dominion. In the case of an inconsistency between a Crown grant of land and aboriginal title, the title should not necessarily give way in the absence of a clear and plain intention to extinguish. In any case, no grants or other interests were granted in the territory prior to 1871, and after that date, the British Columbia legislature had no power to legislate to extinguish, by adverse dominion, or otherwise. Lambert J.A. recognized, at p. 312, that because of s. 91(24) of the *Constitution Act, 1867*, and the doctrine of interjurisdictional immunity, provincial legislation could not affect "Indians in their Indianness". This included aboriginal rights, since they are an integral part of aboriginal culture. This is not affected by s. 88 of the *Indian Act*.

52 Lambert J.A. applied the same principles to a consideration of whether the right to self-government had been extinguished. Neither the assertion of sovereignty nor the colonial enactments mentioned by the trial judge were sufficient to extinguish aboriginal rights in the claimed territory. He saw no incompatibility between statements that the Crown owned the land of the province and the notion that aboriginal title was a burden on the Crown's radical title. Moreover, there was no "inescapable inference" that the colonial enactments were intended to extinguish aboriginal interests. If this were the case, aboriginal peoples would instantly become trespassers on any lands not reserved for them as soon as the Crown took title. Finally, the evidence that the aboriginal peoples of northern British Columbia surrendered their title under Treaty No. 8 also suggested that they had title interests to surrender.

(c) Findings at Trial

53 Lambert J.A. considered the factual findings made by the trial judge and made a number of general observations. First, if a finding of fact is necessary to the decision in the case, it should be given more deference than a fact which is merely made in the course of the decision or for some incidental reason. Second, findings of historical fact based on historical or anthropological evidence given by historians and anthropologists should be given only the kind of weight that other historians or anthropologists

might have given them. These social scientists do not always agree, circumstances change, and new material is discovered and interpreted. Third, the appellants' oral evidence should be weighed, like all evidence, against the weight of countervailing evidence and not against an absolute standard so long as it is enough to support an air of reality. Fourth, with the election of an NDP government in British Columbia in 1991, the province reconsidered its legal stance in this case. As such, it invited the court to confirm the existence of aboriginal rights of unspecified content over unspecified areas and to permit the parties to negotiate the precise content and the precise areas. In Lambert J.A.'s view, the Crown, by adopting the position that it wished to negotiate the content and territorial scope of aboriginal rights, must be taken to have waived the argument that the findings of the trial judge must stand and that any aboriginal rights held by the Gitksan and Wet'suwet'en peoples must be confined to non-exclusive sustenance rights over the area covered by Map 5. In short, reliance on the findings of fact of the trial judge is entirely inconsistent with negotiation.

54 Nonetheless, Lambert J.A. was of the view that the findings of fact with respect to boundaries and with respect to the scope and content of aboriginal rights, including both rights in land and rights of self-government, cannot stand even in accordance with the usual principles governing the consideration of findings of fact, because they are flawed by errors of law.

55 With regard to the ownership claim, Lambert J.A. identified the following errors in the trial judge's reasons. In his view, the trial judge erred: (1) in not treating the ownership claim as a claim to aboriginal title and applied incorrect legal standards as a result; (2) in treating the claim to aboriginal title as a claim to a proprietary interest in land; (3) in applying a test of indefinite or long, long time use and occupation before the assertion of sovereignty; (4) in treating evidence of commercial interaction with the first Europeans as not being evidence of aboriginal practices; (5) in treating the rights to trap as being the exercise of rights other than aboriginal rights; (6) in rejecting evidence about commercial trapping and the evidence of Dr. Ray, a historical geographer who

gave evidence at trial; (7) in rejecting possession, occupation, use, and enjoyment in a social sense as sufficient to establish aboriginal title; (8) in treating the test of possession and occupation as being whether there was a law which would have required a trespasser to depart; (9) in considering that aboriginal rights cannot be held jointly by more than one people; (10) in not concluding that aboriginal title could rest on occupation, possession, use, and enjoyment of land even though that occupation may have diminished in the period after contact; (11) in his treatment of blanket extinguishment of aboriginal title; and (12) in concluding that all aboriginal rights had been extinguished by the colonial instruments. These errors of law led to an incorrect conclusion on the part of the trial judge about the existence of aboriginal title. His findings of fact can be reconsidered on appellate review.

56 With regard to the jurisdiction claim, Lambert J.A. stated that the trial judge erred: (1) in treating the claim to jurisdiction as a claim to govern territory and assert sovereignty over the territory; (2) in trying to define the appellants' claim in terms of the answers given by one witness in cross-examination; (3) in concluding that the claim to jurisdiction must fail because the nature of aboriginal self-government and self-regulation was such that it does not produce a set of binding and enforceable laws; and (4) in considering that the existence of a legislative institution is an essential part of the existence of an aboriginal right to self-government. Because of these errors of law, the trial judge's conclusions were wrong.

57 With regard to the claim to aboriginal rights, Lambert J.A. was of the view that the trial judge erred: (1) in not treating the evidence of occupation, possession, use, and enjoyment of the territory in an organized way by the appellants for their purposes, but particularly for sustenance, as being sufficient to establish aboriginal title to much of the land within the territory; (2) in separating commercial practices of aboriginal people from other practices and saying that commercial practices were not aboriginal practices; (3) in not considering the evidence of trading practices with neighbouring peoples; (4) in his treatment of the question of exclusivity both in relation to aboriginal title and

sustenance rights; and (5) in considering participation in the wage or cash economy in relation to the existence (or non-existence) of aboriginal title. Again, given these errors of law, Lambert J.A. asserted that an appellate court had jurisdiction to intervene and set aside the trial judge's findings.

(d) Substituted Findings

58 In light of these errors, Lambert J.A. substituted his own findings of fact for those of the trial judge. In his view, the evidence established that in 1846, the Gitksan and Wet'suwet'en peoples occupied, possessed, used and enjoyed their traditional ancestral lands in accordance with their own practices, customs and traditions which were an integral part of their distinctive culture. Those ancestral lands extend throughout the claimed territory, well beyond the area indicated in Map 5. In areas where there were no conflicting claims to user rights, the appellants' rights should be characterized as aboriginal title. In areas of shared occupancy and use, the appellants' title would be shared-exclusive aboriginal title. In areas where the Gitksan and Wet'suwet'en peoples did not occupy, possess or use the land as an integral part of their culture, they would not have title, but may have aboriginal sustenance rights. These rights were not extinguished through any blanket extinguishment in the colonial period. Precise legislation related to a specific area may have extinguished some rights. However, no such legislation was before the court. The geographic scope of the rights was a matter to be negotiated between the parties, and failing negotiation, needed to be determined by a new trial.

59 Lambert J.A. also concluded that in 1846, the appellants' ancestors had rights of self-government and self-regulation, which rested on the practices, customs and traditions of those people which formed an integral part of their distinctive cultures. It is true that the rights may have been diminished by the assertion of British sovereignty, but those rights that continue are protected by s. 35 of the *Constitution Act, 1982*.

60 Turning to aboriginal sustenance rights, Lambert J.A. stated that they are entirely encompassed within aboriginal title in those areas where Gitksan and Wet'suwet'en aboriginal title

exists. They also may exist in areas outside of title lands. In areas where such rights were shared by a number of peoples, the appellants' rights may be limited to specific sustenance activities as opposed to exclusive or shared-exclusive use and occupation.

(e) Other Issues

61 With regard to the *Royal Proclamation, 1763*, R.S.C., 1985, App. II, No. 1, Lambert J.A. expressed no views on its application or effect in the claimed territory and its inhabitants. With regard to infringement or denial of the appellants' rights in the claimed territory, Lambert J.A. concluded that the evidence in the case did not permit a proper consideration of the issues. Each infringement or denial would have to be examined in relation to the specific circumstances.

(f) Disposition

62 Lambert J.A. would have allowed the appeal, and made a number of declarations. First, he would declare that the Gitksan and Wet'suwet'en peoples had, at the time of the assertion of British sovereignty in 1846, aboriginal title to occupy, possess, use and enjoy all or some of the land within the claimed territory. The land covered by aboriginal title at that time extended far beyond village sites and the immediate areas surrounding. Second, he would declare that the Gitksan and Wet'suwet'en peoples may have had aboriginal sustenance rights, including hunting, fishing, gathering, and similar rights over any parts of the land within the claimed territory to which aboriginal title did not extend. He would also declare that the aboriginal title and the aboriginal sustenance rights described may have been exclusive to the Gitksan in certain areas and exclusive to the Wet'suwet'en in others, and in some they may have shared with each other, or other aboriginal peoples, or non-aboriginals.

63 Lambert J.A. would have also declared that the appellants' ancestors had, at the time of the assertion of British sovereignty in 1846, aboriginal rights of self-government and self-regulation relating to their own organized society, its members, its institutions and its sustenance rights. These rights were recognized by,

incorporated into, and protected by the common law after 1846. They have not been extinguished by any form of blanket extinguishment. Hence, they exist in modern form, subject only to specific extinguishment of the specific title or specific sustenance right in a specific area. However, the right of aboriginal self-government did not include any rights that were inconsistent with British sovereignty, any rights that are repugnant to natural justice, equity and good conscience, and have not been modified to overcome that repugnancy, and any rights which are contrary to the part of the common law that applied to the territory, the Gitksan and Wet'suwet'en peoples and their institutions.

64 Lambert J.A. would also declare that these aboriginal title rights, aboriginal rights of self-government and self-regulation, and aboriginal sustenance rights may have been subject, after 1846 to specific extinguishment by the clear and plain extinguishing intention of the Sovereign Power, legislatively expressed by Parliament. Any specific extinguishment of specific rights might have been express or implicit, and, if implicit, it may have been brought about by the legislation itself (implied extinguishment) or by acts authorized by the legislation (extinguishment by adverse dominion), provided the intention to extinguish was contained within the legislative expression and was clear and plain. Instances of such specific extinguishment could not be decided on this appeal.

65 Lambert J.A. would declare that the present aboriginal rights of self-government and self-regulation of the Gitksan and Wet'suwet'en peoples, exercisable in relation to their aboriginal title, would include the specific rights claimed in this appeal by the plaintiffs in relation to aboriginal title. He would also declare that the present aboriginal rights of self-government and self-regulation of the Gitksan and Wet'suwet'en peoples would include rights of self-government and self-regulation exercisable through their own institutions to preserve and enhance their social, political, cultural, linguistic and spiritual identity.

66 Finally, Lambert J.A. would remit a number of questions back to trial. These include the question of the territorial boundaries for both title and sustenance rights; the degree of exclusivity

or shared exclusivity which the appellants hold, on both the territories over which they have title and the territories over which they have sustenance rights; the scope and content of the sustenance rights; the scope and content of the rights to self-government and self-regulation; and all questions relating to the plaintiffs' entitlement to damages and the quantum of damages. He would have also awarded the plaintiffs their costs, both in the Court of Appeal, and at trial.

(4) *Hutcheon J.A. (dissenting in part)*
(a) Rights to Land

67 Hutcheon J.A. agreed with the trial judge that the *Royal Proclamation, 1763* did not apply to the territory or its inhabitants. Nonetheless, the policy reflected in the *Proclamation* was, generally speaking, acceptance of aboriginal rights to land. Moreover, Hutcheon J.A. concluded on the basis of *Calder* and *Sparrow* that the colonial enactments did not extinguish the aboriginal rights in the claimed territory. He found it unnecessary to decide whether a grant in fee simple extinguishes aboriginal title or whether entitlement to compensation arises in such circumstances.

(b) Nature of the Rights

68 Hutcheon J.A. accepted that aboriginal rights to land existed prior to 1846 over the claimed territory. He found it sufficient to say, at p. 389, that aboriginal rights can "compete on an equal footing" with proprietary interests. Additionally, he noted that these rights are collective, inalienable except to the Crown, and extend to the traditional territory of the particular people.

(c) Territory

69 Hutcheon J.A. disagreed with the trial judge's conclusion that the appellants' ancestors occupied or controlled only the villages in the territory and the immediately surrounding areas. In Hutcheon J.A.'s view, the trial judge misapprehended the legal test for occupation and disregarded the independent evidence which showed that the territory occupied or controlled by the appellants extended far beyond the villages.

(d) Self-Regulation

70 The traditions of the Gitksan and Wet'suwet'en peoples existed long before 1846 and continued thereafter. They included the right to names and titles, the use of masks and symbols in rituals, the use of ceremonial robes, and the right to occupy and control places of economic importance. The traditions also included the institution of the clans and the Houses in which membership descended through the mother and the feast system. They regulated marriage and relations with neighbouring societies. The right to practise these traditions was not lost, although the *Indian Act* and provincial laws have affected the appellants' right to self-regulation. Only negotiations will define with greater specificity the areas and terms under which the appellants and the federal and provincial governments will exercise jurisdiction in respect of the appellants, their institutions, and laws.

(e) Disposition

71 Hutcheon J.A. would have allowed the appeal and have made a number of declarations. First, he would declare that all of the aboriginal rights of the appellants were not extinguished before 1871. Second, the appellants continue to have existing aboriginal rights to undefined portions of land within the claimed territory. Third, the appellants have rights of self-regulation exercisable through their own institutions to preserve and enhance their social, political, cultural, linguistic and spiritual identity. He would have remitted the outstanding matters to the Supreme Court of British Columbia, and stayed the proceedings for two years from the date of the judgment, or such shorter or longer period, in order for the parties to agree about the lands in respect of which the appellants have aboriginal rights, the scope of such rights on and to such lands, the scope of the right of self-regulation, and the appellants' entitlement to and quantum of damages. Hutcheon J.A. would have awarded the appellants their costs throughout the proceedings.

IV. Issues

72 The following are the principal issues which must be addressed in this appeal. As will become apparent in my analysis,

some of these issues in turn raise a number of sub-issues which I will address as well:

A. Do the pleadings preclude the Court from entertaining claims for aboriginal title and self-government?
B. What is the ability of this Court to interfere with the factual findings made by the trial judge?
C. What is the content of aboriginal title, how is it protected by s. 35(1) of the *Constitution Act, 1982*, and what is required for its proof?
D. Has a claim to self-government been made out by the appellants?
E. Did the province have the power to extinguish aboriginal rights after 1871, either under its own jurisdiction or through the operation of s. 88 of the *Indian Act*?

V. Analysis
A. *Do the Pleadings Preclude the Court from Entertaining Claims for Aboriginal Title and Self-government?*

73 In their pleadings, the appellants, 51 Chiefs representing most of the Houses of the Gitksan and Wet'suwet'en nations, originally advanced 51 individual claims on their own behalf and on behalf of their Houses for "ownership" and "jurisdiction" over 133 distinct territories which together comprise 58,000 square kilometres of northwestern British Columbia. On appeal, that original claim was altered in two different ways. First, the claims for ownership and jurisdiction have been replaced with claims for aboriginal title and self-government, respectively. Second, the individual claims by each house have been amalgamated into two communal claims, one advanced on behalf of each nation. However, there were no formal amendments to the pleadings to this effect, and the respondents accordingly argue that claims which are central to this appeal are not properly before the Court. Furthermore, the respondents argue that they have suffered prejudice as a result because they might have conducted the defence quite differently had they known the case to meet.

74 I reject the respondents' submission with respect to the

substitution of aboriginal title and self-government for the original claims of ownership and jurisdiction. Although it is true that the pleadings were not formally amended, the trial judge, at p. 158, did allow a *de facto* amendment to permit "a claim for aboriginal rights other than ownership and jurisdiction". Had the respondents been concerned about the prejudice arising from this ruling, they could have appealed accordingly. However, they did not, and, as a result, the decision of the trial judge on this point must stand.

75 Moreover, in my opinion, that ruling was correct because it was made against the background of considerable legal uncertainty surrounding the nature and content of aboriginal rights, under both the common law and s. 35(1). The content of common law aboriginal title, for example, has not been authoritatively determined by this Court and has been described by some as a form of "ownership". As well, this case was pleaded prior to this Court's decision in *Sparrow, supra*, which was the first statement from this Court on the types of rights that come within the scope of s. 35(1). The law has rapidly evolved since then. Accordingly, it was just and appropriate for the trial judge to allow for an amendment to pleadings which were framed when the jurisprudence was in its infancy.

76 However, no such amendment was made with respect to the amalgamation of the individual claims brought by the 51 Gitksan and Wet'suwet'en Houses into two collective claims, one by each nation, for aboriginal title and self-government. Given the absence of an amendment to the pleadings, I must reluctantly conclude that the respondents suffered some prejudice. The appellants argue that the respondents did not experience prejudice since the collective and individual claims are related to the extent that the territory claimed by each nation is merely the sum of the individual claims of each House; the external boundaries of the collective claims therefore represent the outer boundaries of the outer territories. Although that argument carries considerable weight, it does not address the basic point that the collective claims were simply not in issue at trial. To frame the case in a different manner on appeal would retroactively deny the respondents the opportunity to know the appellants' case.

77 This defect in the pleadings prevents the Court from considering the merits of this appeal. However, given the importance of this case and the fact that much of the evidence of individual territorial holdings is extremely relevant to the collective claims now advanced by each of the appellants, the correct remedy for the defect in pleadings is a new trial, where, to quote the trial judge at p. 368, "[i]t will be for the parties to consider whether any amendment is required in order to make the pleadings conform with the evidence". Moreover, as I will now explain, there are other reasons why a new trial should be ordered.

B. *What is the Ability of this Court to Interfere with the Factual Findings Made by the Trial Judge?*

(1) *General Principles*

78 I recently reviewed the principles governing the appellate review of findings of fact in *Van der Peet, supra*. As a general rule, this Court has been extremely reluctant to interfere with the findings of fact made at trial, especially when those findings of fact are based on an assessment of the testimony and credibility of witnesses. Unless there is a "palpable and overriding error", appellate courts should not substitute their own findings of fact for those of the trial judge. The leading statement of this principle can be found in *Stein v. The Ship "Kathy K"*, [1976] 2 S.C.R. 802, *per* Ritchie J., at p. 808:

These authorities are not to be taken as meaning that the findings of fact made at trial are immutable, but rather that they are not to be reversed unless it can be established that the learned trial judge made some palpable and overriding error which affected his assessment of the facts. While the Court of Appeal is seized with the duty of re-examining the evidence in order to be satisfied that no such error occurred, it is not, in my view, a part of its function to substitute its assessment of the balance of probability for the findings of the judge who presided at the trial.

The same deference must be accorded to the trial judge's assessment of the credibility of expert witnesses: see *N.V. Bocimar S.A. v. Century Insurance Co. of Canada*, [1987] 1 S.C.R. 1247.

79 The policy reason underlying this rule is protection of "[t]he autonomy and integrity of the trial process" (*Schwartz v. Canada*, [1996] 1 S.C.R. 254, at p. 278), which recognizes that the trier of fact, who is in direct contact with the mass of the evidence, is in the best position to make findings of fact, particularly those which turn on credibility. Moreover, *Van der Peet* clarified that deference was owed to findings of fact even when the trial judge misapprehended the law which was applied to those facts, a problem which can arise in quickly evolving areas of law such as the jurisprudence surrounding s. 35(1).

80 I recently held, in *Van der Peet*, that these general principles apply to cases litigated under s. 35(1). On the other hand, while accepting the general principle of non-interference, this Court has also identified specific situations in which an appeal court can interfere with a finding of fact made at trial. For example, appellate intervention is warranted "where the courts below have misapprehended or overlooked material evidence": see *Chartier v. Attorney General of Quebec*, [1979] 2 S.C.R. 474, at p. 493. In cases involving the determination of aboriginal rights, appellate intervention is also warranted by the failure of a trial court to appreciate the evidentiary difficulties inherent in adjudicating aboriginal claims when, first, applying the rules of evidence and, second, interpreting the evidence before it. As I said in *Van der Peet*, at para. 68:

In determining whether an aboriginal claimant has produced evidence sufficient to demonstrate that her activity is an aspect of a practice, custom or tradition integral to a distinctive aboriginal culture, a court should approach the rules of evidence, and interpret the evidence that exists, with a consciousness of the special nature of aboriginal claims, and of the evidentiary difficulties in proving a right which originates in times where there were no written records of the practices, customs and traditions engaged in. The courts must not undervalue the evidence presented by aboriginal claimants simply because that evidence does not conform precisely with the evidentiary standards that would be applied in, for example, a private law torts case.

81 The justification for this special approach can be found in the nature of aboriginal rights themselves. I explained in *Van der*

Peet that those rights are aimed at the reconciliation of the prior occupation of North America by distinctive aboriginal societies with the assertion of Crown sovereignty over Canadian territory. They attempt to achieve that reconciliation by "their bridging of aboriginal and non-aboriginal cultures" (at para. 42). Accordingly, "a court must take into account the perspective of the aboriginal people claiming the right. . . . while at the same time taking into account the perspective of the common law" such that "[t]rue reconciliation will, equally, place weight on each" (at paras. 49 and 50).

82 In other words, although the doctrine of aboriginal rights is a common law doctrine, aboriginal rights are truly *sui generis*, and demand a unique approach to the treatment of evidence which accords due weight to the perspective of aboriginal peoples. However, that accommodation must be done in a manner which does not strain "the Canadian legal and constitutional structure" (at para. 49). Both the principles laid down in *Van der Peet*—first, that trial courts must approach the rules of evidence in light of the evidentiary difficulties inherent in adjudicating aboriginal claims, and second, that trial courts must interpret that evidence in the same spirit—must be understood against this background.

83 A concrete application of the first principle can be found in *Van der Peet* itself, where I addressed the difficulties inherent in demonstrating a continuity between current aboriginal activities and the pre-contact practices, customs and traditions of aboriginal societies. As I reiterate below, the requirement for continuity is one component of the definition of aboriginal rights (although, as I explain below, in the case of title, the issue is continuity from sovereignty, not contact). However, given that many aboriginal societies did not keep written records at the time of contact or sovereignty, it would be exceedingly difficult for them to produce (at para. 62) "conclusive evidence from pre-contact times about the practices, customs and traditions of their community". Accordingly, I held that (at para. 62):

The evidence relied upon by the applicant and the courts may relate to aboriginal practices, customs and traditions *post-contact*; it simply needs to be directed at demonstrating which aspects of the aboriginal community and society have their origins *pre-contact*. [Emphasis added.]

The same considerations apply when the time from which title is determined is sovereignty.

84 This appeal requires us to apply not only the first principle in *Van der Peet* but the second principle as well, and adapt the laws of evidence so that the aboriginal perspective on their practices, customs and traditions and on their relationship with the land, are given due weight by the courts. In practical terms, this requires the courts to come to terms with the oral histories of aboriginal societies, which, for many aboriginal nations, are the only record of their past. Given that the aboriginal rights recognized and affirmed by s. 35(1) are defined by reference to pre-contact practices or, as I will develop below, in the case of title, pre-sovereignty occupation, those histories play a crucial role in the litigation of aboriginal rights.

85 A useful and informative description of aboriginal oral history is provided by the *Report of the Royal Commission on Aboriginal Peoples* (1996), vol. 1 (*Looking Forward, Looking Back*), at p. 33:

The Aboriginal tradition in the recording of history is neither linear nor steeped in the same notions of social progress and evolution [as in the non-Aboriginal tradition]. Nor is it usually human-centred in the same way as the western scientific tradition, for it does not assume that human beings are anything more than one—and not necessarily the most important—element of the natural order of the universe. Moreover, the Aboriginal historical tradition is an oral one, involving legends, stories and accounts handed down through the generations in oral form. It is less focused on establishing objective truth and assumes that the teller of the story is so much a part of the event being described that it would be arrogant to presume to classify or categorize the event exactly or for all time.

In the Aboriginal tradition the purpose of repeating oral accounts from the past is broader than the role of written history in western societies. It may be to educate the listener, to communicate aspects of culture, to socialize people into a cultural tradition, or to validate the claims of a particular family to authority and prestige....

Oral accounts of the past include a good deal of subjective experience. They are not simply a detached recounting of factual events but, rather, are "facts enmeshed in the stories of a lifetime". They are also likely to be rooted in particular locations, making reference to particular families and communities. This contributes to a sense that there are many histories, each characterized in part by how a people see themselves, how they define their identity in relation to their environment, and how they express their uniqueness as a people.

86 Many features of oral histories would count against both their admissibility and their weight as evidence of prior events in a court that took a traditional approach to the rules of evidence. The most fundamental of these is their broad social role not only "as a repository of historical knowledge for a culture" but also as an expression of "the values and mores of [that] culture": Clay McLeod, "The Oral Histories of Canada's Northern People, Anglo-Canadian Evidence Law, and Canada's Fiduciary Duty to First Nations: Breaking Down the Barriers of the Past" (1992), 30 *Alta. L. Rev.* 1276, at p. 1279. Dickson J. (as he then was) recognized as much when he stated in *Kruger v. The Queen*, [1978] 1 S.C.R. 104, at p. 109, that "[c]laims to aboriginal title are woven with history, legend, politics and moral obligations." The difficulty with these features of oral histories is that they are tangential to the ultimate purpose of the fact-finding process at trial—the determination of the historical truth. Another feature of oral histories which creates difficulty is that they largely consist of out-of-court statements, passed on through an unbroken chain across the generations of a particular aboriginal nation to the present-day. These out-of-court statements are admitted for their truth and therefore conflict with the general rule against the admissibility of hearsay.

87 Notwithstanding the challenges created by the use of oral histories as proof of historical facts, the laws of evidence must be adapted in order that this type of evidence can be accommodated and placed on an equal footing with the types of historical evidence that courts are familiar with, which largely consists of historical documents. This is a long-standing practice in the interpretation of treaties between the Crown and aboriginal peoples: *Sioui, supra,* at p. 1068; *R. v. Taylor* (1981), 62 C.C.C. (2d) 227 (Ont. C.A.), at

p. 232. To quote Dickson C.J., given that most aboriginal societies "did not keep written records", the failure to do so would "impose an impossible burden of proof" on aboriginal peoples, and "render nugatory" any rights that they have (*Simon v. The Queen*, [1985] 2 S.C.R. 387, at p. 408). This process must be undertaken on a case-by-case basis. I will take this approach in my analysis of the trial judge's findings of fact.

88 On a final note, it is important to understand that even when a trial judge has erred in making a finding of fact, appellate intervention does not proceed automatically. The error must be sufficiently serious that it was "overriding and determinative in the assessment of the balance of probabilities with respect to that factual issue" (*Schwartz, supra*, at p. 281).

(2) *Application of General Principles*
(a) General Comments
89 The general principle of appellate non-interference applies with particular force in this appeal. The trial was lengthy and very complex. There were 318 days of testimony. There were a large number of witnesses, lay and expert. The volume of evidence is enormous. To quote the trial judge at pp. 116–17:

A total of 61 witnesses gave evidence at trial, many using translators from their native Gitksan or Wet'suwet'en language; "word spellers" to assist the official reporters were required for many witnesses; a further 15 witnesses gave their evidence on commission; 53 territorial affidavits were filed; 30 deponents were cross-examined out of court; there are 23,503 pages of transcript evidence at trial; 5,898 pages of transcript of argument; 3,039 pages of commission evidence and 2,553 pages of cross-examination on affidavits (all evidence and oral arguments are conveniently preserved in hard copy and on diskettes); about 9,200 exhibits were filed at trial comprising, I estimate, well over 50,000 pages; the plaintiffs' draft outline of argument comprises 3,250 pages, the province's 1,975 pages, and Canada's over 1,000 pages; there are 5,977 pages of transcript of argument in hard copy and on diskettes. All parties filed some excerpts from the exhibits they referred to in argument. The province alone submitted 28 huge binders of such documents. At least 15 binders of reply argument were left with me during that stage of the trial.

The result was a judgment of over 400 pages in length.

90 It is not open to the appellants to challenge the trial judge's findings of fact merely because they disagree with them. I fear that a significant number of the appellants' objections fall into this category. Those objections are too numerous to list in their entirety. The bulk of these objections, at best, relate to alleged instances of misapprehension or oversight of material evidence by the trial judge. However, the respondents have established that, in most situations, there was *some* contradictory evidence that supported the trial judge's conclusion. The question, ultimately, was one of weight, and the appellants have failed to demonstrate that the trial judge erred in this respect.

91 One objection that I would like to mention specifically, albeit in passing, is the trial judge's refusal to accept the testimony of two anthropologists who were brought in as expert witnesses by the appellants. This aspect of the trial judge's reasons was hotly contested by the appellants in their written submissions. However, I need only reiterate what I have stated above, that findings of credibility, including the credibility of expert witnesses, are for the trial judge to make, and should warrant considerable deference from appellate courts.

92 On the other hand, the appellants have alleged that the trial judge made a number of serious errors relating to the treatment of the oral histories of the appellants. Those oral histories were expressed in three different forms: (i) the *adaawk* of the Gitksan, and the *kungax* of the Wet'suwet'en; (ii) the personal recollections of members of the appellant nations, and (iii) the territorial affidavits filed by the heads of the individual houses within each nation. The trial judge ruled on both the admissibility of, and the weight to be given to, these various forms of oral history without the benefit of my reasons in *Van der Peet*, as will become evident in the discussion that follows.

(b) *Adaawk* and *Kungax*

93 The *adaawk* and *kungax* of the Gitksan and Wet'suwet'en nations, respectively, are oral histories of a special kind. They were described by the trial judge, at p. 164, as a "sacred 'official' litany, or

history, or recital of the most important laws, history, traditions and traditional territory of a House". The content of these special oral histories includes in its physical representation totem poles, crests and blankets. The importance of the *adaawk* and *kungax* is underlined by the fact that they are "repeated, performed and authenticated at important feasts" (at p. 164). At those feasts, dissenters have the opportunity to object if they question any detail and, in this way, help ensure the authenticity of the *adaawk* and *kungax*. Although they serve largely the same role, the trial judge found that there are some differences in both the form and content of the *adaawk* and the *kungax*. For example, the latter is "in the nature of a song ... which is intended to represent the special authority and responsibilities of a chief...." However, these differences are not legally relevant for the purposes of the issue at hand.

94 It is apparent that the *adaawk* and *kungax* are of integral importance to the distinctive cultures of the appellant nations. At trial, they were relied on for two distinct purposes. First, the *adaawk* was relied on as a component of and, therefore, as proof of the existence of a system of land tenure law internal to the Gitksan, which covered the whole territory claimed by that appellant. In other words, it was offered as evidence of the Gitksan's historical use and occupation of that territory. For the Wet'-suwet'en, the *kungax* was offered as proof of the central significance of the claimed lands to their distinctive culture. As I shall explain later in these reasons, both use and occupation, and the central significance of the lands occupied, are relevant to proof of aboriginal title.

95 The admissibility of the *adaawk* and *kungax* was the subject of a general decision of the trial judge handed down during the course of the trial regarding the admissibility of all oral histories (incorrectly indexed as *Uukw v. R.*, [1987] 6 W.W.R. 155 (B.C.S.C.)). Although the trial judge recognized that the evidence at issue was a form of hearsay, he ruled it admissible on the basis of the recognized exception that declarations made by deceased persons could be given in evidence by witnesses as proof of public or general rights: see Michael N. Howard, Peter Crane

and Daniel A. Hochberg, *Phipson on Evidence* (14th ed. 1990), at p. 736. He affirmed that earlier ruling in his trial judgment, correctly in my view, by stating, at p. 180, that the *adaawk* and *kungax* were admissible "out of necessity as exceptions to the hearsay rule" because there was no other way to prove the history of the Gitksan and Wet'suwet'en nations.

96 The trial judge, however, went on to give these oral histories no independent weight at all. He held, at p. 180, that they were only admissible as "direct evidence of facts in issue ... in a few cases where they could constitute confirmatory proof of early presence in the territory". His central concern that the *adaawk* and *kungax* could not serve "as evidence of detailed history, or land ownership, use or occupation". I disagree with some of the reasons he relied on in support of this conclusion.

97 Although he had earlier recognized, when making his ruling on admissibility, that it was impossible to make an easy distinction between the mythological and "real" aspects of these oral histories, he discounted the *adaawk* and *kungax* because they were not "literally true", confounded "what is fact and what is belief", "included some material which might be classified as mythology", and projected a "romantic view" of the history of the appellants. He also cast doubt on the authenticity of these special oral histories (at p. 181) because, *inter alia*, "the verifying group is so small that they cannot safely be regarded as expressing the reputation of even the Indian community, let alone the larger community whose opportunity to dispute territorial claims would be essential to weight". Finally, he questioned (at p. 181) the utility of the *adaawk* and *kungax* to demonstrate use and occupation because they were "seriously lacking in detail about the specific lands to which they are said to relate".

98 Although he framed his ruling on weight in terms of the specific oral histories before him, in my respectful opinion, the trial judge in reality based his decision on some general concerns with the use of oral histories as evidence in aboriginal rights cases. In summary, the trial judge gave no independent weight to these special oral histories because they did not accurately convey historical truth, because knowledge about those oral histories was

confined to the communities whose histories they were and because those oral histories were insufficiently detailed. However, as I mentioned earlier, these are features, to a greater or lesser extent, of all oral histories, not just the *adaawk* and *kungax*. The implication of the trial judge's reasoning is that oral histories should never be given any independent weight and are only useful as confirmatory evidence in aboriginal rights litigation. I fear that if this reasoning were followed, the oral histories of aboriginal peoples would be consistently and systematically undervalued by the Canadian legal system, in contradiction of the express instruction to the contrary in *Van der Peet* that trial courts interpret the evidence of aboriginal peoples in light of the difficulties inherent in adjudicating aboriginal claims.

(c) Recollections of Aboriginal Life

99 The trial judge also erred when he discounted the "recollections of aboriginal life" offered by various members of the appellant nations. I take that term to be a reference to testimony about personal and family history that is not part of an *adaawk* or a *kungax*. That evidence consisted of the personal knowledge of the witnesses and declarations of witnesses' ancestors as to land use. This history had been adduced by the appellants in order to establish the requisite degree of use and occupation to make out a claim to ownership and, for the same reason as the *adaawk* and *kungax*, is material to the proof of aboriginal title.

100 The trial judge limited the uses to which the evidence could be put. He reasoned, at p. 177, that this evidence, at most, established "without question, that the plaintiff's immediate ancestors, for the past 100 years or so" had used land in the claimed territory for aboriginal purposes. However, the evidence was insufficiently precise to demonstrate that the more distant ancestors of the witnesses had engaged in specific enough land use "far enough back in time to permit the plaintiffs to succeed on issues such as internal boundaries". In the language of *Van der Peet*, the trial judge effectively held that this evidence did not demonstrate the requisite continuity between present occupation and past occupation in order to ground a claim for aboriginal title.

101 In my opinion, the trial judge expected too much of the oral history of the appellants, as expressed in the recollections of aboriginal life of members of the appellant nations. He expected that evidence to provide definitive and precise evidence of pre-contact aboriginal activities on the territory in question. However, as I held in *Van der Peet*, this will be almost an impossible burden to meet. Rather, if oral history cannot conclusively establish pre-sovereignty (after this decision) occupation of land, it may still be relevant to demonstrate that current occupation has its origins prior to sovereignty. This is exactly what the appellants sought to do.

(d) Territorial Affidavits

102 Finally, the trial judge also erred in his treatment of the territorial affidavits filed by the appellant chiefs. Those affidavits were declarations of the territorial holdings of each of the Gitksan and Wet'suwet'en houses and, at trial, were introduced for the purposes of establishing each House's ownership of its specific territory. Before this Court, the appellants tried to amalgamate these individual claims into collective claims on behalf of each nation and the relevance of the affidavits changed accordingly. I have already held that it is not open to the appellants to alter fundamentally the nature of their claim in this way on appeal. Nevertheless, the treatment of the affidavits is important because they will be relevant at a new trial to the existence and nature of the land tenure system within each nation and, therefore, material to the proof of title.

103 The affidavits rely heavily on the declarations of deceased persons of use or ownership of the lands, which are a form of oral history. But those declarations are a kind of hearsay and the appellants therefore argued that the affidavits should be admitted through the reputation exception to the hearsay rule. Although he recognized, at p. 438, that the territorial affidavits were "the best evidence [the appellants] could adduce on this question of internal boundaries", the trial judge held that this exception did not apply and refused to admit the declarations contained in the affidavits.

104 I am concerned by the specific reasons the trial judge gave for refusing to apply the reputation exception. He questioned the degree to which the declarations amounted to a reputation because they were largely confined to the appellants' communities. The trial judge asserted that neighbouring aboriginal groups whose territorial claims conflicted with those of the appellants, as well as non-aboriginals who potentially possessed a legal interest in the claimed territory, were unaware of the content of the alleged reputation at all. Furthermore, the trial judge reasoned that since the subject-matter of the affidavits was disputed, its reliability was doubtful. Finally, the trial judge questioned, at p. 441, "the independence and objectivity" of the information contained in the affidavits, because the appellants and their ancestors (at p. 440) "have been actively discussing land claims for many years".

105 Although he regretted this finding, the trial judge felt bound to apply the rules of evidence because it did not appear to him (at p. 442) "that the Supreme Court of Canada has decided that the ordinary rules of evidence do not apply to this kind of case". The trial judge arrived at this conclusion, however, without the benefit of *Van der Peet*, where I held that the ordinary rules of evidence must be approached and adapted in light of the evidentiary difficulties inherent in adjudicating aboriginal claims.

106 Many of the reasons relied on by the trial judge for excluding the evidence contained in the territorial affidavits are problematic because they run against this fundamental principle. The requirement that a reputation be known in the general community, for example, ignores the fact that oral histories, as noted by the *Royal Commission on Aboriginal Peoples*, generally relate to particular locations, and refer to particular families and communities and may, as a result, be unknown outside of that community, even to other aboriginal nations. Excluding the territorial affidavits because the claims to which they relate are disputed does not acknowledge that claims to aboriginal rights, and aboriginal title in particular, are almost always disputed and contested. Indeed, if those claims were uncontroversial, there would be no need to bring them to the courts for resolution. Casting doubt on the

reliability of the territorial affidavits because land claims had been actively discussed for many years also fails to take account of the special context surrounding aboriginal claims, in two ways. First, those claims have been discussed for so long because of British Columbia's persistent refusal to acknowledge the existence of aboriginal title in that province until relatively recently, largely as a direct result of the decision of this Court in *Calder, supra*. It would be perverse, to say the least, to use the refusal of the province to acknowledge the rights of its aboriginal inhabitants as a reason for excluding evidence which may prove the existence of those rights. Second, this rationale for exclusion places aboriginal claimants whose societies record their past through oral history in a grave dilemma. In order for the oral history of a community to amount to a form of reputation, and to be admissible in court, it must remain alive through the discussions of members of that community; those discussions are the very basis of that reputation. But if those histories are discussed too much, and too close to the date of litigation, they may be discounted as being suspect, and may be held to be inadmissible. The net effect may be that a society with such an oral tradition would never be able to establish a historical claim through the use of oral history in court.

(e) Conclusion

107 The trial judge's treatment of the various kinds of oral histories did not satisfy the principles I laid down in *Van der Peet*. These errors are particularly worrisome because oral histories were of critical importance to the appellants' case. They used those histories in an attempt to establish their occupation and use of the disputed territory, an essential requirement for aboriginal title. The trial judge, after refusing to admit, or giving no independent weight to these oral histories, reached the conclusion that the appellants had not demonstrated the requisite degree of occupation for "ownership". Had the trial judge assessed the oral histories correctly, his conclusions on these issues of fact might have been very different.

108 In the circumstances, the factual findings cannot stand. However, given the enormous complexity of the factual issues at

hand, it would be impossible for the Court to do justice to the parties by sifting through the record itself and making new factual findings. A new trial is warranted, at which the evidence may be considered in light of the principles laid down in *Van der Peet* and elaborated upon here. In applying these principles, the new trial judge might well share some or all of the findings of fact of McEachern C.J.

C. *What is the Content of Aboriginal Title, How is it Protected by s. 35(1) of the Constitution Act, 1982, and What is Required for its Proof?*

(1) *Introduction*

109 The parties disagree over whether the appellants have established aboriginal title to the disputed area. However, since those factual issues require a new trial, we cannot resolve that dispute in this appeal. But factual issues aside, the parties also have a more fundamental disagreement over the content of aboriginal title itself, and its reception into the Constitution by s. 35(1). In order to give guidance to the judge at the new trial, it is to this issue that I will now turn.

110 I set out these opposing positions by way of illustration and introduction because I believe that all of the parties have characterized the content of aboriginal title incorrectly. The appellants argue that aboriginal title is tantamount to an inalienable fee simple, which confers on aboriginal peoples the rights to use those lands as they choose and which has been constitutionalized by s. 35(1). The respondents offer two alternative formulations: first, that aboriginal title is no more than a bundle of rights to engage in activities which are themselves aboriginal rights recognized and affirmed by s. 35(1), and that the *Constitution Act, 1982,* merely constitutionalizes those individual rights, not the bundle itself, because the latter has no independent content; and second, that aboriginal title, at most, encompasses the right to exclusive use and occupation of land in order to engage in those activities which are aboriginal rights themselves, and that s. 35(1) constitutionalizes this notion of exclusivity.

111 The content of aboriginal title, in fact, lies somewhere in

between these positions. Aboriginal title is a right in land and, as such, is more than the right to engage in specific activities which may be themselves aboriginal rights. Rather, it confers the right to use land for a variety of activities, not all of which need be aspects of practices, customs and traditions which are integral to the distinctive cultures of aboriginal societies. Those activities do not constitute the right *per se*; rather, they are parasitic on the underlying title. However, that range of uses is subject to the limitation that they must not be irreconcilable with the nature of the attachment to the land which forms the basis of the particular group's aboriginal title. This inherent limit, to be explained more fully below, flows from the definition of aboriginal title as a *sui generis* interest in land, and is one way in which aboriginal title is distinct from a fee simple.

(2) *Aboriginal Title at Common Law*
(a) General Features

112 The starting point of the Canadian jurisprudence on aboriginal title is the Privy Council's decision in *St. Catherine's Milling and Lumber Co. v. The Queen* (1888), 14 A.C. 46, which described aboriginal title as a "personal and usufructuary right" (at p. 54). The subsequent jurisprudence has attempted to grapple with this definition, and has in the process demonstrated that the Privy Council's choice of terminology is not particularly helpful to explain the various dimensions of aboriginal title. What the Privy Council sought to capture is that aboriginal title is a *sui generis* interest in land. Aboriginal title has been described as *sui generis* in order to distinguish it from "normal" proprietary interests, such as fee simple. However, as I will now develop, it is also *sui generis* in the sense that its characteristics cannot be completely explained by reference either to the common law rules of real property or to the rules of property found in aboriginal legal systems. As with other aboriginal rights, it must be understood by reference to both common law and aboriginal perspectives.

113 The idea that aboriginal title is *sui generis* is the unifying principle underlying the various dimensions of that title. One dimension is its *inalienability*. Lands held pursuant to aboriginal

title cannot be transferred, sold or surrendered to anyone other than the Crown and, as a result, is inalienable to third parties. This Court has taken pains to clarify that aboriginal title is only "personal" in this sense, and does not mean that aboriginal title is a non-proprietary interest which amounts to no more than a licence to use and occupy the land and cannot compete on an equal footing with other proprietary interests: see *Canadian Pacific Ltd. v. Paul*, [1988] 2 S.C.R. 654, at p. 677.

114 Another dimension of aboriginal title is its *source*. It had originally been thought that the source of aboriginal title in Canada was the *Royal Proclamation, 1763*: see *St. Catherine's Milling*. However, it is now clear that although aboriginal title was recognized by the *Proclamation*, it arises from the prior occupation of Canada by aboriginal peoples. That prior occupation, however, is relevant in two different ways, both of which illustrate the *sui generis* nature of aboriginal title. The first is the physical fact of occupation, which derives from the common law principle that occupation is proof of possession in law: see Kent McNeil, *Common Law Aboriginal Title* (1989), at p. 7. Thus, in *Guerin, supra*, Dickson J. described aboriginal title, at p. 376, as a "legal right derived from the Indians' historic occupation and possession of their tribal lands". What makes aboriginal title *sui generis* is that it arises from possession *before* the assertion of British sovereignty, whereas normal estates, like fee simple, arise afterward: see Kent McNeil, "The Meaning of Aboriginal Title", in Michael Asch, ed., *Aboriginal and Treaty Rights in Canada* (1997), 135, at p. 144. This idea has been further developed in *Roberts v. Canada*, [1989] 1 S.C.R. 322, where this Court unanimously held at p. 340 that "aboriginal title pre-dated colonization by the British and survived British claims of sovereignty" (also see *Guerin*, at p. 378). What this suggests is a second source for aboriginal title—the relationship between common law and pre-existing systems of aboriginal law.

115 A further dimension of aboriginal title is the fact that it is held *communally*. Aboriginal title cannot be held by individual aboriginal persons; it is a collective right to land held by all members of an aboriginal nation. Decisions with respect to that land

are also made by that community. This is another feature of aboriginal title which is *sui generis* and distinguishes it from normal property interests.

(b) The Content of Aboriginal Title

116 Although cases involving aboriginal title have come before this Court and Privy Council before, there has never been a definitive statement from either court on the *content* of aboriginal title. In *St. Catherine's Milling*, the Privy Council, as I have mentioned, described the aboriginal title as a "personal and usufructuary right", but declined to explain what that meant because it was not "necessary to express any opinion upon the point" (at p. 55). Similarly, in *Calder*, *Guerin*, and *Paul*, the issues were the extinguishment of, the fiduciary duty arising from the surrender of, and statutory easements over land held pursuant to, aboriginal title, respectively; the content of title was not at issue and was not directly addressed.

117 Although the courts have been less than forthcoming, I have arrived at the conclusion that the content of aboriginal title can be summarized by two propositions: first, that aboriginal title encompasses the right to exclusive use and occupation of the land held pursuant to that title for a variety of purposes, which need not be aspects of those aboriginal practices, customs and traditions which are integral to distinctive aboriginal cultures; and second, that those protected uses must not be irreconcilable with the nature of the group's attachment to that land. For the sake of clarity, I will discuss each of these propositions separately.

Aboriginal title encompasses the right to use the land held pursuant to that title for a variety of purposes, which need not be aspects of those aboriginal practices, cultures and traditions which are integral to distinctive aboriginal cultures

118 The respondents argue that aboriginal title merely encompasses the right to engage in activities which are aspects of aboriginal practices, customs and traditions which are integral to distinctive aboriginal cultures of the aboriginal group claiming the right and, at most, adds the notion of exclusivity; i.e., the exclusive right to use the land for those purposes. However, the uses

to which lands held pursuant to aboriginal title can be put are not restricted in this way. This conclusion emerges from three sources: (i) the Canadian jurisprudence on aboriginal title, (ii) the relationship between reserve lands and lands held pursuant to aboriginal title, and (iii) the *Indian Oil and Gas Act*, R.S.C., 1985, c. I-7. As well, although this is not legally determinative, it is supported by the critical literature. In particular, I have profited greatly from Professor McNeil's article, "The Meaning of Aboriginal Title", *supra*.

(i) Canadian jurisprudence on aboriginal title

119 Despite the fact that the jurisprudence on aboriginal title is somewhat underdeveloped, it is clear that the uses to which lands held pursuant to aboriginal title can be put is not restricted to the practices, customs and traditions of aboriginal peoples integral to distinctive aboriginal cultures. In *Guerin*, for example, Dickson J. described aboriginal title as an "interest in land" which encompassed "a legal right to occupy and possess certain lands" (at p. 382). The "right to occupy and possess" is framed in broad terms and, significantly, is not qualified by reference to traditional and customary uses of those lands. Any doubt that the right to occupancy and possession encompasses a broad variety of uses of land was put to rest in *Paul*, where the Court went even further and stated that aboriginal title was "more than the right to enjoyment and occupancy" (at p. 678). Once again, there is no reference to aboriginal practices, customs and traditions as a qualifier on that right. Moreover, I take the reference to "more" as emphasis of the broad notion of use and possession.

(ii) Reserve land

120 Another source of support for the conclusion that the uses to which lands held under aboriginal title can be put are not restricted to those grounded in practices, customs and traditions integral to distinctive aboriginal cultures can be found in *Guerin*, where Dickson J. stated at p. 379 that the same legal principles governed the aboriginal interest in reserve lands and lands held pursuant to aboriginal title:

It does not matter, in my opinion, that the present case is concerned with the interest of an Indian Band in a reserve rather than with unrecognized aboriginal title in traditional tribal lands. *The Indian interest in the land is the same in both cases.* [Emphasis added.]

121 The nature of the Indian interest in reserve land is very broad, and can be found in s. 18 of the *Indian Act*, which I reproduce in full:

18. (1) Subject to this Act, reserves are held by Her Majesty for the *use and benefit* of the respective bands for which they were set apart, and subject to this Act and to the terms of any treaty or surrender, the Governor in Council may determine whether any purpose for which lands in a reserve are used or are to be used is for the use and benefit of the band.

(2) The Minister may authorize the use of lands in a reserve for the purpose of Indian schools, the administration of Indian affairs, Indian burial grounds, Indian health projects or, with the consent of the council of the band, *for any other purpose for the general welfare of the band*, and may take any lands in a reserve required for those purposes, but where an individual Indian, immediately prior to the taking, was entitled to the possession of those lands, compensation for that use shall be paid to the Indian, in such amount as may be agreed between the Indian and the Minister, or, failing agreement, as may be determined in such manner as the Minister may direct. [Emphasis added.]

The principal provision is s. 18(1), which states that reserve lands are held "for the use and benefit" of the bands which occupy them; those uses and benefits, on the face of the *Indian Act*, do not appear to be restricted to practices, customs and traditions integral to distinctive aboriginal cultures. The breadth of those uses is reinforced by s. 18(2), which states that reserve lands may be used "for any other purpose for the general welfare of the band". The general welfare of the band has not been defined in terms of aboriginal practices, customs and traditions, nor in terms of those activities which have their origin pre-contact; it is a concept, by definition, which incorporates a reference to the present-day needs of aboriginal communities. On the basis of *Guerin*, lands held pursuant to aboriginal title, like reserve lands, are also capable of being used for a broad variety of purposes.

(iii) *Indian Oil and Gas Act*

122 The third source for the proposition that the content of aboriginal title is not restricted to practices, customs and traditions which are integral to distinctive aboriginal cultures is the *Indian Oil and Gas Act*. The overall purpose of the statute is to provide for the exploration of oil and gas on reserve lands through their surrender to the Crown. The statute presumes that the aboriginal interest in reserve land includes mineral rights, a point which this Court unanimously accepted with respect to the *Indian Act* in *Blueberry River Indian Band v. Canada (Department of Indian Affairs and Northern Development)*, [1995] 4 S.C.R. 344. On the basis of *Guerin*, aboriginal title also encompasses mineral rights, and lands held pursuant to aboriginal title should be capable of exploitation in the same way, which is certainly not a traditional use for those lands. This conclusion is reinforced by s. 6(2) of the *Act*, which provides:

(2) Nothing in this Act shall be deemed to abrogate the rights of Indian people or preclude them from negotiating for oil and gas benefits in those areas in which land claims have not been settled.

The areas referred to in s. 6(2), at the very least, must encompass lands held pursuant to aboriginal title, since those lands by definition have not been surrendered under land claims agreements. The presumption underlying s. 6(2) is that aboriginal title permits the development of oil and gas reserves.

123 Although this is not determinative, the conclusion that the content of aboriginal title is not restricted to those uses with their origins in the practices, customs and traditions integral to distinctive aboriginal societies has wide support in the critical literature: Jocelyn Gagne, "The Content of Aboriginal Title at Common Law: A Look at the Nishga Claim" (1982–83), 47 *Sask. L. Rev.* 309 at pp. 336–37; Kent McNeil, *Common Law Aboriginal Title, supra,* at p. 242; Kent McNeil, "The Meaning of Aboriginal Title", *supra,*

at pp. 143–150; William Pentney, "The Rights of the Aboriginal Peoples of Canada in the *Constitution Act, 1982* Part II—Section 35: The Substantive Guarantee" (1988), 22 *U.B.C. L. Rev.* 207, at p. 221; *Report of the Royal Commission on Aboriginal Peoples*, vol. 2 (*Restructuring the Relationship*), at p. 561; Brian Slattery, "The Constitutional Guarantee of Aboriginal and Treaty Rights" (1982–83), 8 *Queen's L.J.* 232, at pp. 268–9; Brian Slattery, *Ancestral Lands, Alien Laws: Judicial Perspectives on Aboriginal Title* (1983), at p. 34; Brian Slattery, "Understanding Aboriginal Rights", 66 *Can. Bar Rev.* 727, at pp. 746–48.

124 In conclusion, the content of aboriginal title is not restricted to those uses which are elements of a practice, custom or tradition integral to the distinctive culture of the aboriginal group claiming the right. However, nor does aboriginal title amount to a form of inalienable fee simple, as I will now explain.

(c) Inherent Limit: Lands Held Pursuant to Aboriginal Title Cannot Be Used in a Manner that Is Irreconcilable with the Nature of the Attachment to the Land Which Forms the Basis of the Group's Claim to Aboriginal Title

125 The content of aboriginal title contains an inherent limit that lands held pursuant to title cannot be used in a manner that is irreconcilable with the nature of the claimants' attachment to those lands. This limit on the content of aboriginal title is a manifestation of the principle that underlies the various dimensions of that special interest in land—it is a *sui generis* interest that is distinct from "normal" proprietary interests, most notably fee simple.

126 I arrive at this conclusion by reference to the other dimensions of aboriginal title which are *sui generis* as well. I first consider the source of aboriginal title. As I discussed earlier, aboriginal title arises from the prior occupation of Canada by aboriginal peoples. That prior occupation is relevant in two different ways: first, because of the physical fact of occupation, and second, because aboriginal title originates in part from pre-existing systems of aboriginal law. However, the law of aboriginal title does not only seek to determine the historic rights of aboriginal peoples to land;

it also seeks to afford legal protection to prior occupation in the present-day. Implicit in the protection of historic patterns of occupation is a recognition of the importance of the continuity of the relationship of an aboriginal community to its land over time.

127 I develop this point below with respect to the test for aboriginal title. The relevance of the continuity of the relationship of an aboriginal community with its land here is that it applies not only to the past, but to the future as well. That relationship should not be prevented from continuing into the future. As a result, uses of the lands that would threaten that future relationship are, by their very nature, excluded from the content of aboriginal title.

128 Accordingly, in my view, lands subject to aboriginal title cannot be put to such uses as may be irreconcilable with the nature of the occupation of that land and the relationship that the particular group has had with the land which together have given rise to aboriginal title in the first place. As discussed below, one of the critical elements in the determination of whether a particular aboriginal group has aboriginal title to certain lands is the matter of the occupancy of those lands. Occupancy is determined by reference to the activities that have taken place on the land and the uses to which the land has been put by the particular group. If lands are so occupied, there will exist a special bond between the group and the land in question such that the land will be part of the definition of the group's distinctive culture. It seems to me that these elements of aboriginal title create an inherent limitation on the uses to which the land, over which such title exists, may be put. For example, if occupation is established with reference to the use of the land as a hunting ground, then the group that successfully claims aboriginal title to that land may not use it in such a fashion as to destroy its value for such a use (e.g., by strip mining it). Similarly, if a group claims a special bond with the land because of its ceremonial or cultural significance, it may not use the land in such a way as to destroy that relationship (e.g., by developing it in such a way that the bond is destroyed, perhaps by turning it into a parking lot).

129 It is for this reason also that lands held by virtue of aboriginal title may not be alienated. Alienation would bring to an end

the entitlement of the aboriginal people to occupy the land and would terminate their relationship with it. I have suggested above that the inalienability of aboriginal lands is, at least in part, a function of the common law principle that settlers in colonies must derive their title from Crown grant and, therefore, cannot acquire title through purchase from aboriginal inhabitants. It is also, again only in part, a function of a general policy "to ensure that Indians are not dispossessed of their entitlements": see *Mitchell v. Peguis Indian Band*, [1990] 2 S.C.R. 85, at p. 133. What the inalienability of lands held pursuant to aboriginal title suggests is that those lands are more than just a fungible commodity. The relationship between an aboriginal community and the lands over which it has aboriginal title has an important non-economic component. The land has an inherent and unique value in itself, which is enjoyed by the community with aboriginal title to it. The community cannot put the land to uses which would destroy that value.

130 I am cognizant that the *sui generis* nature of aboriginal title precludes the application of "traditional real property rules" to elucidate the content of that title (*St. Mary's Indian Band v. Cranbrook (City)*, [1997] 2 S.C.R. 657, at para. 14). Nevertheless, a useful analogy can be drawn between the limit on aboriginal title and the concept of equitable waste at common law. Under that doctrine, persons who hold a life estate in real property cannot commit "wanton or extravagant acts of destruction" (E. H. Burn, *Cheshire and Burn's Modern Law of Real Property* (14th ed. 1988), at p. 264) or "ruin the property" (Robert E. Megarry and H. W. R. Wade, *The Law of Real Property* (4th ed. 1975), at p. 105). This description of the limits imposed by the doctrine of equitable waste captures the kind of limit I have in mind here.

131 Finally, what I have just said regarding the importance of the continuity of the relationship between an aboriginal community and its land, and the non-economic or inherent value of that land, should not be taken to detract from the possibility of surrender to the Crown in exchange for valuable consideration. On the contrary, the idea of surrender reinforces the conclusion that aboriginal title is limited in the way I have described. If

aboriginal peoples wish to use their lands in a way that aboriginal title does not permit, then they must surrender those lands and convert them into non-title lands to do so.

132 The foregoing amounts to a general limitation on the use of lands held by virtue of aboriginal title. It arises from the particular physical and cultural relationship that a group may have with the land and is defined by the source of aboriginal title over it. This is not, I must emphasize, a limitation that restricts the use of the land to those activities that have traditionally been carried out on it. That would amount to a legal straitjacket on aboriginal peoples who have a legitimate legal claim to the land. The approach I have outlined above allows for a full range of uses of the land, subject only to an overarching limit, defined by the special nature of the aboriginal title in that land.

(d) Aboriginal Title under s. 35(1) of the Constitution Act, 1982

133 Aboriginal title at common law is protected in its full form by s. 35(1). This conclusion flows from the express language of s. 35(1) itself, which states in full: "[t]he *existing* aboriginal and treaty rights of the aboriginal peoples of Canada are hereby recognized and affirmed" (emphasis added). On a plain reading of the provision, s. 35(1) did not create aboriginal rights; rather, it accorded constitutional status to those rights which were "existing" in 1982. The provision, at the very least, constitutionalized those rights which aboriginal peoples possessed at common law, since those rights existed at the time s. 35(1) came into force. Since aboriginal title was a common law right whose existence was recognized well before 1982 (e.g., *Calder, supra*), s. 35(1) has constitutionalized it in its full form.

134 I expressed this understanding of the relationship between common law aboriginal rights, including aboriginal title, and the aboriginal rights protected by s. 35(1) in *Van der Peet*. While explaining the purposes behind s. 35(1), I stated that "it must be remembered that s. 35(1) did not create the legal doctrine of aboriginal rights; aboriginal rights existed and were recognized under the common law" (at para. 28). Through the enactment of s. 35(1), "a pre-existing legal doctrine was elevated to constitutional status"

(at para. 29), or in other words, s. 35(1) had achieved "the constitutionalization of those rights" (at para. 29).

135 Finally, this view of the effect of s. 35(1) on common law aboriginal title is supported by numerous commentators: Patrick Macklem, "First Nations Self-Government and the Borders of the Canadian Legal Imagination" (1991), 36 *McGill L.J.* 382, at pp. 447–48; Kent McNeil, "The Constitutional Rights of the Aboriginal Peoples of Canada" (1982), 4 *Sup. Ct. L. Rev.* 255, at pp. 256–57; James O'Reilly, "La *Loi constitutionnelle de 1982*, droit des autochtones" (1984), 25 *C. de D.* 125, at p. 137; William Pentney, "The Rights of the Aboriginal Peoples of Canada in the *Constitution Act, 1982* Part II—Section 35: The Substantive Guarantee", *supra*, at pp. 220–21; Douglas Sanders, "The Rights of the Aboriginal Peoples of Canada" (1983), 61 *Can. Bar Rev.* 314, at p. 329; Douglas Sanders, "Pre-Existing Rights: The Aboriginal Peoples of Canada", in Gérald-A. Beaudoin and Ed Ratushny, eds., *The Canadian Charter of Rights and Freedoms* (2nd ed. 1989), 707, at pp. 731–32; Brian Slattery, "The Constitutional Guarantee of Aboriginal and Treaty Rights", *supra*, at p. 254; Brian Slattery, *Ancestral Lands, Alien Laws: Judicial Perspectives on Aboriginal Title, supra*, at p. 45.

136 I hasten to add that the constitutionalization of common law aboriginal rights by s. 35(1) does not mean that those rights exhaust the content of s. 35(1). As I said in *Côté, supra*, at para. 52:

Section 35(1) would fail to achieve its noble purpose of preserving the integral and defining features of distinctive aboriginal societies if it only protected those defining features which were fortunate enough to have received the legal recognition and approval of European colonizers.

I relied on this proposition in *Côté* to defeat the argument that the possible absence of aboriginal rights under French colonial law was a bar to the existence of aboriginal rights under s. 35(1) within the historic boundaries of New France. But it also follows that the existence of a particular aboriginal right at common law is not a *sine qua non* for the proof of an aboriginal right that is recognized and affirmed by s. 35(1). Indeed, none of the decisions of this

Court handed down under s. 35(1) in which the existence of an aboriginal right has been demonstrated has relied on the existence of that right at common law. The existence of an aboriginal right at common law is therefore sufficient, but not necessary, for the recognition and affirmation of that right by s. 35(1).

137 The acknowledgement that s. 35(1) has accorded constitutional status to common law aboriginal title raises a further question—the relationship of aboriginal title to the "aboriginal rights" protected by s. 35(1). I addressed that question in *Adams*, *supra*, where the Court had been presented with two radically different conceptions of this relationship. The first conceived of aboriginal rights as being "inherently based in aboriginal title to the land" (at para. 25), or as fragments of a broader claim to aboriginal title. By implication, aboriginal rights must rest either in a claim to title or the unextinguished remnants of title. Taken to its logical extreme, this suggests that aboriginal title is merely the sum of a set of individual aboriginal rights, and that it therefore has no independent content. However, I rejected this position for another—that aboriginal title is "simply one manifestation of a broader-based conception of aboriginal rights" (at para. 25). Thus, although aboriginal title is a species of aboriginal right recognized and affirmed by s. 35(1), it is distinct from other aboriginal rights because it arises where the connection of a group with a piece of land "was of a central significance to their distinctive culture" (at para. 26).

138 The picture which emerges from *Adams* is that the aboriginal rights which are recognized and affirmed by s. 35(1) fall along a spectrum with respect to their degree of connection with the land. At the one end, there are those aboriginal rights which are practices, customs and traditions that are integral to the distinctive aboriginal culture of the group claiming the right. However, the *"occupation and use of the land"* where the activity is taking place is not *"sufficient to support a claim of title to the land"* (at para. 26 (emphasis in original)). Nevertheless, those activities receive constitutional protection. In the middle, there are activities which, out of necessity, take place on land and indeed, might be intimately related to a particular piece of land. Although an

aboriginal group may not be able to demonstrate title to the land, it may nevertheless have a site-specific right to engage in a particular activity. I put the point this way in *Adams*, at para. 30:

Even where an aboriginal right exists on a tract of land to which the aboriginal people in question do not have title, that right may well be site specific, with the result that it can be exercised only upon that specific tract of land. For example, if an aboriginal people demonstrates that hunting on a specific tract of land was an integral part of their distinctive culture then, even if the right exists apart from title to that tract of land, the aboriginal right to hunt is nonetheless defined as, and limited to, the right to hunt on the specific tract of land.

At the other end of the spectrum, there is aboriginal title itself. As *Adams* makes clear, aboriginal title confers more than the right to engage in site-specific activities which are aspects of the practices, customs and traditions of distinctive aboriginal cultures. Site-specific rights can be made out even if title cannot. What aboriginal title confers is the right to the land itself.

139 Because aboriginal rights can vary with respect to their degree of connection with the land, some aboriginal groups may be unable to make out a claim to title, but will nevertheless possess aboriginal rights that are recognized and affirmed by s. 35(1), including site-specific rights to engage in particular activities. As I explained in *Adams*, this may occur in the case of nomadic peoples who varied "the location of their settlements with the season and changing circumstances" (at para. 27). The fact that aboriginal peoples were non-sedentary, however (at para. 27) "does not alter the fact that nomadic peoples survived through reliance on the land prior to contact with Europeans and, further, that many of the practices, customs and traditions of nomadic peoples that took place on the land were integral to their distinctive cultures."

(e) Proof of Aboriginal Title
(i) Introduction

140 In addition to differing in the degree of connection with the land, aboriginal title differs from other aboriginal rights in

another way. To date, the Court has defined aboriginal rights in terms of *activities*. As I said in *Van der Peet* (at para. 46):

[I]n order to be an aboriginal right an *activity* must be an element of a practice, custom or tradition integral to the distinctive culture of the aboriginal group claiming the right. [Emphasis added.]

Aboriginal title, however, is a *right to the land itself.* Subject to the limits I have laid down above, that land may be used for a variety of activities, none of which need be individually protected as aboriginal rights under s. 35(1). Those activities are parasitic on the underlying title.

141 This difference between aboriginal rights to engage in particular activities and aboriginal title requires that the test I laid down in *Van der Peet* be adapted accordingly. I anticipated this possibility in *Van der Peet* itself, where I stated that (at para. 74):

Aboriginal rights arise from the prior occupation of land, but they also arise from the prior social organization and distinctive cultures of aboriginal peoples on that land. In considering whether a claim to an aboriginal right has been made out, courts must look at both the relationship of an aboriginal claimant to the land and at the practices, customs and traditions arising from the claimant's distinctive culture and society. Courts must not focus so entirely on the relationship of aboriginal peoples with the land that they lose sight of the other factors relevant to the identification and definition of aboriginal rights.

Since the purpose of s. 35(1) is to reconcile the prior presence of aboriginal peoples in North America with the assertion of Crown sovereignty, it is clear from this statement that s. 35(1) must recognize and affirm both aspects of that prior presence—first, the occupation of land, and second, the prior social organization and distinctive cultures of aboriginal peoples on that land. To date the jurisprudence under s. 35(1) has given more emphasis to the second aspect. To a great extent, this has been a function of the types of cases which have come before this Court under s. 35(1)—

prosecutions for regulatory offences that, by their very nature, proscribe discrete types of activity.

142 The adaptation of the test laid down in *Van der Peet* to suit claims to title must be understood as the recognition of the first aspect of that prior presence. However, as will now become apparent, the tests for the identification of aboriginal rights to engage in particular activities and for the identification of aboriginal title share broad similarities. The major distinctions are first, under the test for aboriginal title, the requirement that the land be integral to the distinctive culture of the claimants is subsumed by the requirement of occupancy, and second, whereas the time for the identification of aboriginal rights is the time of first contact, the time for the identification of aboriginal title is the time at which the Crown asserted sovereignty over the land.

(ii) The test for the proof of aboriginal title

143 In order to make out a claim for aboriginal title, the aboriginal group asserting title must satisfy the following criteria: (i) the land must have been occupied prior to sovereignty, (ii) if present occupation is relied on as proof of occupation pre-sovereignty, there must be a continuity between present and pre-sovereignty occupation, and (iii) at sovereignty, that occupation must have been exclusive.

The land must have been occupied prior to sovereigntly.

144 In order to establish a claim to aboriginal title, the aboriginal group asserting the claim must establish that it occupied the lands in question at the *time at which the Crown asserted sovereignty over the land subject to the title*. The relevant time period for the establishment of title is, therefore, different than for the establishment of aboriginal rights to engage in specific activities. In *Van der Peet*, I held, at para. 60 that "[t]he time period that a court should consider in identifying whether the right claimed meets the standard of being integral to the aboriginal community claiming the right is the period prior to contact...." This arises from the fact that in defining the central and distinctive attributes of pre-existing aboriginal societies it is necessary to look to a time prior to the arrival of Europeans. Practices, customs or traditions

that arose solely as a response to European influences do not meet the standard for recognition as aboriginal rights.

145 On the other hand, in the context of aboriginal title, sovereignty is the appropriate time period to consider for several reasons. First, from a theoretical standpoint, aboriginal title arises out of prior occupation of the land by aboriginal peoples and out of the relationship between the common law and pre-existing systems of aboriginal law. Aboriginal title is a burden on the Crown's underlying title. However, the Crown did not gain this title until it asserted sovereignty over the land in question. Because it does not make sense to speak of a burden on the underlying title before that title existed, aboriginal title crystallized at the time sovereignty was asserted. Second, aboriginal title does not raise the problem of distinguishing between distinctive, integral aboriginal practices, customs and traditions and those influenced or introduced by European contact. Under common law, the act of occupation or possession is sufficient to ground aboriginal title and it is not necessary to prove that the land was a distinctive or integral part of the aboriginal society before the arrival of Europeans. Finally, from a practical standpoint, it appears that the date of sovereignty is more certain than the date of first contact. It is often very difficult to determine the precise moment that each aboriginal group had first contact with European culture. I note that this is the approach that has support in the academic literature: Brian Slattery, "Understanding Aboriginal Rights", *supra*, at p. 742; Kent McNeil, *Common Law Aboriginal Title, supra*, at p. 196. For these reasons, I conclude that aboriginals must establish occupation of the land from the date of the assertion of sovereignty in order to sustain a claim for aboriginal title. McEachern C.J. found, at pp. 233–34, and the parties did not dispute on appeal, that British sovereignty over British Columbia was conclusively established by the *Oregon Boundary Treaty* of 1846. This is not to say that circumstances subsequent to sovereignty may never be relevant to title or compensation; this might be the case, for example, where native bands have been dispossessed of traditional lands after sovereignty.

146 There was a consensus among the parties on appeal that

proof of historic occupation was required to make out a claim to aboriginal title. However, the parties disagreed on how that occupancy could be proved. The respondents assert that in order to establish aboriginal title, the occupation must be the physical occupation of the land in question. The appellant Gitksan nation argue, by contrast, that aboriginal title may be established, at least in part, by reference to aboriginal law.

147 This debate over the proof of occupancy reflects two divergent views of the source of aboriginal title. The respondents argue, in essence, that aboriginal title arises from the physical reality at the time of sovereignty, whereas the Gitksan effectively take the position that aboriginal title arises from and should reflect the pattern of land holdings under aboriginal law. However, as I have explained above, the source of aboriginal title appears to be grounded both in the common law and in the aboriginal perspective on land; the latter includes, but is not limited to, their systems of law. It follows that both should be taken into account in establishing the proof of occupancy. Indeed, there is precedent for doing so. In *Baker Lake, supra,* Mahoney J. held that to prove aboriginal title, the claimants needed both to demonstrate their "physical presence on the land they occupied" (at p. 561) and the existence "among [that group of] . . . a recognition of the claimed rights. . . . by the regime that prevailed before" (at p. 559).

148 This approach to the proof of occupancy at common law is also mandated in the context of s. 35(1) by *Van der Peet.* In that decision, as I stated above, I held at para. 50 that the reconciliation of the prior occupation of North America by aboriginal peoples with the assertion of Crown sovereignty required that account be taken of the "aboriginal perspective while at the same time taking into account the perspective of the common law" and that "[t]rue reconciliation will, equally, place weight on each". I also held that the aboriginal perspective on the occupation of their lands can be gleaned, in part, but not exclusively, from their traditional laws, because those laws were elements of the practices, customs and traditions of aboriginal peoples: at para. 41. As a result, if, at the time of sovereignty, an aboriginal society had laws in relation to land, those laws would be relevant to establishing the occupation

of lands which are the subject of a claim for aboriginal title. Relevant laws might include, but are not limited to, a land tenure system or laws governing land use.

149 However, the aboriginal perspective must be taken into account alongside the perspective of the common law. Professor McNeil has convincingly argued that at common law, the fact of physical occupation is proof of possession at law, which in turn will ground title to the land: *Common Law Aboriginal Title, supra,* at p. 73; also see *Cheshire and Burn's Modern Law of Real Property, supra,* at p. 28; and Megarry and Wade, *The Law of Real Property, supra,* at p. 1006. Physical occupation may be established in a variety of ways, ranging from the construction of dwellings through cultivation and enclosure of fields to regular use of definite tracts of land for hunting, fishing or otherwise exploiting its resources: see McNeil, *Common Law Aboriginal Title,* at pp. 201–2. In considering whether occupation sufficient to ground title is established, "one must take into account the group's size, manner of life, material resources, and technological abilities, and the character of the lands claimed": Brian Slattery, "Understanding Aboriginal Rights", *supra,* at p. 758.

150 In *Van der Peet,* I drew a distinction between those practices, customs and traditions of aboriginal peoples which were "an aspect of, or took place in" the society of the aboriginal group asserting the claim and those which were "a central and significant part of the society's distinctive culture" (at para. 55). The latter stood apart because they "made the culture of the society distinctive ... it was one of the things that truly *made the society what it was*" (at para. 55, emphasis in original). The same requirement operates in the determination of the proof of aboriginal title. As I said in *Adams,* a claim to title is made out when a group can demonstrate "that their connection with the piece of land ... was of a central significance to their distinctive culture" (at para. 26).

151 Although this remains a crucial part of the test for aboriginal rights, given the occupancy requirement in the test for aboriginal title, I cannot imagine a situation where this requirement would actually serve to limit or preclude a title claim. The requirement exists for rights short of title because it is necessary to

distinguish between those practices which were central to the culture of claimants and those which were more incidental. However, in the case of title, it would seem clear that any land that was occupied pre-sovereignty, and which the parties have maintained a substantial connection with since then, is sufficiently important to be of central significance to the culture of the claimants. As a result, I do not think it is necessary to include explicitly this element as part of the test for aboriginal title.

If present occupation is relied on as proof of occupation presovereignty, there must be a continuity between present and presovereignty occupation

152 In *Van der Peet*, I explained that it is the pre-contact practices, customs and traditions of aboriginal peoples which are recognized and affirmed as aboriginal rights by s. 35(1). But I also acknowledged it would be "next to impossible" (at para. 62) for an aboriginal group to provide conclusive evidence of its pre-contact practices, customs and traditions. What would suffice instead was evidence of post-contact practices, which was "directed at demonstrating which aspects of the aboriginal community and society have their origins pre-contact" (at para. 62). The same concern, and the same solution, arises with respect to the proof of occupation in claims for aboriginal title, although there is a difference in the time for determination of title. Conclusive evidence of pre-sovereignty occupation may be difficult to come by. Instead, an aboriginal community may provide evidence of present occupation as proof of pre-sovereignty occupation in support of a claim to aboriginal title. What is required, in addition, is a *continuity* between present and pre-sovereignty occupation, because the relevant time for the determination of aboriginal title is at the time before sovereignty.

153 Needless to say, there is no need to establish "an unbroken chain of continuity" (*Van der Peet*, at para. 65) between present and prior occupation. The occupation and use of lands may have been disrupted for a time, perhaps as a result of the unwillingness of European colonizers to recognize aboriginal title. To impose the requirement of continuity too strictly would risk "undermining the very purpose of s. 35(1) by perpetuating the historical injustice

suffered by aboriginal peoples at the hands of colonizers who failed to respect" aboriginal rights to land (*Côté, supra,* at para. 53). In *Mabo, supra,* the High Court of Australia set down the requirement that there must be "substantial maintenance of the connection" between the people and the land. In my view, this test should be equally applicable to proof of title in Canada.

154 I should also note that there is a strong possibility that the precise nature of occupation will have changed between the time of sovereignty and the present. I would like to make it clear that the fact that the nature of occupation has changed would not ordinarily preclude a claim for aboriginal title, as long as a substantial connection between the people and the land is maintained. The only limitation on this principle might be the internal limits on uses to which land subject to aboriginal title may be put: i.e., uses which are inconsistent with continued use by future generations of aboriginals.

At sovereignty, occupation must have been exclusive

155 Finally, at sovereignty, occupation must have been exclusive. The requirement for exclusivity flows from the definition of aboriginal title itself, because I have defined aboriginal title in terms of the right to *exclusive* use and occupation of land. Exclusivity, as an aspect of aboriginal title, vests in the aboriginal community which holds the ability to exclude others from the lands held pursuant to that title. The proof of title must, in this respect, mirror the content of the right. Were it possible to prove title without demonstrating exclusive occupation, the result would be absurd, because it would be possible for more than one aboriginal nation to have aboriginal title over the same piece of land, and then for all of them to attempt to assert the right to exclusive use and occupation over it.

156 As with the proof of occupation, proof of exclusivity must rely on both the perspective of the common law and the aboriginal perspective, placing equal weight on each. At common law, a premium is placed on the factual reality of occupation, as encountered by the Europeans. However, as the common law concept of possession must be sensitive to the realities of aboriginal society, so must the concept of exclusivity. Exclusivity is a common law

principle derived from the notion of fee simple ownership and should be imported into the concept of aboriginal title with caution. As such, the test required to establish exclusive occupation must take into account the context of the aboriginal society at the time of sovereignty. For example, it is important to note that exclusive occupation can be demonstrated even if other aboriginal groups were present, or frequented the claimed lands. Under those circumstances, exclusivity would be demonstrated by "the intention and capacity to retain exclusive control" (McNeil, *Common Law Aboriginal Title*, *supra*, at p. 204). Thus, an act of trespass, if isolated, would not undermine a general finding of exclusivity, if aboriginal groups intended to and attempted to enforce their exclusive occupation. Moreover, as Professor McNeil suggests, the presence of other aboriginal groups might actually reinforce a finding of exclusivity. For example, "[w]here others were allowed access upon request, the very fact that permission was asked for and given would be further evidence of the group's exclusive control" (at p. 204).

157 A consideration of the aboriginal perspective may also lead to the conclusion that trespass by other aboriginal groups does not undermine, and that presence of those groups by permission may reinforce, the exclusive occupation of the aboriginal group asserting title. For example, the aboriginal group asserting the claim to aboriginal title may have trespass laws which are proof of exclusive occupation, such that the presence of trespassers does not count as evidence against exclusivity. As well, aboriginal laws under which permission may be granted to other aboriginal groups to use or reside even temporarily on land would reinforce the finding of exclusive occupation. Indeed, if that permission were the subject of treaties between the aboriginal nations in question, those treaties would also form part of the aboriginal perspective.

158 In their submissions, the appellants pressed the point that requiring proof of exclusive occupation might preclude a finding of joint title, which is shared between two or more aboriginal nations. The possibility of joint title has been recognized by American courts: *United States v. Santa Fe Pacific Railroad Co.*, 314 U.S. 339 (1941). I would suggest that the requirement of exclusive occupancy and the possibility of joint title could be reconciled by

recognizing that joint title could arise from shared exclusivity. The meaning of shared exclusivity is well-known to the common law. Exclusive possession is the right to exclude others. Shared exclusive possession is the right to exclude others except those with whom possession is shared. There clearly may be cases in which two aboriginal nations lived on a particular piece of land and recognized each other's entitlement to that land but nobody else's. However, since no claim to joint title has been asserted here, I leave it to another day to work out all the complexities and implications of joint title, as well as any limits that another band's title may have on the way in which one band uses its title lands.

159 I should also reiterate that if aboriginals can show that they occupied a particular piece of land, but did not do so exclusively, it will always be possible to establish aboriginal rights short of title. These rights will likely be intimately tied to the land and may permit a number of possible uses. However, unlike title, they are not a right to the land itself. Rather, as I have suggested, they are a right to do certain things in connection with that land. If, for example, it were established that the lands near those subject to a title claim were used for hunting by a number of bands, those shared lands would not be subject to a claim for aboriginal title, as they lack the crucial element of exclusivity. However, they may be subject to site-specific aboriginal rights by all of the bands who used it. This does not entitle anyone to the land itself, but it may entitle all of the bands who hunted on the land to hunting rights. Hence, in addition to shared title, it will be possible to have shared, non-exclusive, site-specific rights. In my opinion, this accords with the general principle that the common law should develop to recognize aboriginal rights (and title, when necessary) as they were recognized by either *de facto* practice or by the aboriginal system of governance. It also allows sufficient flexibility to deal with this highly complex and rapidly evolving area of the law.

(f) Infringements of Aboriginal Title: The Test of Justification
(i) Introduction
160 The aboriginal rights recognized and affirmed by s. 35(1), including aboriginal title, are not absolute. Those rights may be

infringed, both by the federal (e.g., *Sparrow*) and provincial (e.g., *Côté*) governments. However, s. 35(1) requires that those infringements satisfy the test of justification. In this section, I will review the Court's nascent jurisprudence on justification and explain how that test will apply in the context of infringements of aboriginal title.

(ii) General principles

161 The test of justification has two parts, which I shall consider in turn. First, the infringement of the aboriginal right must be in furtherance of a legislative objective that is compelling and substantial. I explained in *Gladstone* that compelling and substantial objectives were those which were directed at either one of the purposes underlying the recognition and affirmation of aboriginal rights by s. 35(1), which are (at para. 72):

the recognition of the prior occupation of North America by aboriginal peoples or ... the reconciliation of aboriginal prior occupation with the assertion of the sovereignty of the Crown.

I noted that the latter purpose will often "be most relevant" (at para. 72) at the stage of justification. I think it important to repeat why (at para. 73) that is so:

Because ... distinctive aboriginal societies exist within, and are a part of, a broader social, political and economic community, over which the Crown is sovereign, there are circumstances in which, in order to pursue objectives of compelling and substantial importance to that community as a whole (taking into account the fact that aboriginal societies are a part of that community), some limitation of those rights will be justifiable. Aboriginal rights are a necessary part of the reconciliation of aboriginal societies with the broader political community of which they are part; limits placed on those rights are, where the objectives furthered by those limits are of sufficient importance to the broader community as a whole, equally a necessary part of that reconciliation.

The conservation of fisheries, which was accepted as a compelling and substantial objective in *Sparrow*, furthers both of these purposes, because it simultaneously recognizes that fishing is integral to many aboriginal cultures, and also seeks to reconcile aboriginal societies with the broader community by ensuring that there are fish enough for all. But legitimate government objectives also include "the pursuit of economic and regional fairness" and "the recognition of the historical reliance upon, and participation in, the fishery by non-aboriginal groups" (para. 75). By contrast, measures enacted for relatively unimportant reasons, such as sports fishing without a significant economic component (*Adams*, *supra*) would fail this aspect of the test of justification.

162 The second part of the test of justification requires an assessment of whether the infringement is consistent with the special fiduciary relationship between the Crown and aboriginal peoples. What has become clear is that the requirements of the fiduciary duty are a function of the "legal and factual context" of each appeal (*Gladstone*, *supra*, at para. 56). *Sparrow* and *Gladstone*, for example, interpreted and applied the fiduciary duty in terms of the idea of *priority*. The theory underlying that principle is that the fiduciary relationship between the Crown and aboriginal peoples demands that aboriginal interests be placed first. However, the fiduciary duty does not demand that aboriginal rights always be given priority. As was said in *Sparrow*, *supra*, at pp. 1114–15:

The nature of the constitutional protection afforded by s. 35(1) in this context demands that there be a link between the question of justification and the allocation of priorities in the fishery.

Other contexts permit, and may even require, that the fiduciary duty be articulated in other ways (*Sparrow*, *supra*, at p. 1119):

Within the analysis of justification, there are further questions to be addressed, depending on the circumstances of the inquiry. These include the questions of whether there has been as little infringement as possible in order to effect the desired result; whether, in a situation of expropriation, fair compensation is available; and, whether the aboriginal group in question has been consulted with respect to the conservation measures being implemented.

Sparrow did not explain when the different articulations of the fiduciary duty should be used. Below, I suggest that the choice between them will in large part be a function of the nature of the aboriginal right at issue.

163 In addition to variation in the *form* which the fiduciary duty takes, there will also be variation in degree of scrutiny required by the fiduciary duty of the infringing measure or action. The degree of scrutiny is a function of the nature of the aboriginal right at issue. The distinction between *Sparrow* and *Gladstone*, for example, turned on whether the right amounted to the exclusive use of a resource, which in turn was a function of whether the right had an internal limit. In *Sparrow*, the right was internally limited, because it was a right to fish for food, ceremonial and social purposes, and as a result would only amount to an exclusive right to use the fishery in exceptional circumstances. Accordingly, the requirement of priority was applied strictly to mean that (at p. 1116) "any allocation of priorities after valid conservation measures have been implemented must give top priority to Indian food fishing".

164 In *Gladstone*, by contrast, the right to sell fish commercially was only limited by supply and demand. Had the test for justification been applied in a strict form in *Gladstone*, the aboriginal right would have amounted to an exclusive right to exploit the fishery on a commercial basis. This was not the intention of *Sparrow*, and I accordingly modified the test for justification, by altering the idea of priority in the following way (at para. 62):

the doctrine of priority requires that the government demonstrate that, in allocating the resource, it has taken account of the existence of aboriginal rights and allocated the resource in a manner respectful of the fact that those rights have priority over the exploitation of the fishery by other users. This right is at once both procedural and substantive; at the stage of justification the government must demonstrate both that the process by which it allocated the resource and the actual allocation of the resource which results from that process reflect the prior interest of aboriginal rights holders in the fishery.

After *Gladstone*, in the context of commercial activity, the priority of aboriginal rights is constitutionally satisfied if the government had taken those rights into account and has allocated a resource "in a manner respectful" (at para. 62) of that priority. A court must be satisfied that "the government has taken into account the existence and importance of [aboriginal] rights" (at para. 63) which it determines by asking the following questions (at para. 64):

Questions relevant to the determination of whether the government has granted priority to aboriginal rights holders are ... questions such as whether the government has accommodated the exercise of the aboriginal right to participate in the fishery (through reduced licence fees, for example), whether the government's objectives in enacting a particular regulatory scheme reflect the need to take into account the priority of aboriginal rights holders, the extent of the participation in the fishery of aboriginal rights holders relative to their percentage of the population, how the government has accommodated different aboriginal rights in a particular fishery (food *versus* commercial rights, for example), how important the fishery is to the economic and material well-being of the band in question, and the criteria taken into account by the government in, for example, allocating commercial licences amongst different users.

(iii) Justification and aboriginal title

165 The general principles governing justification laid down in *Sparrow*, and embellished by *Gladstone*, operate with respect to infringements of aboriginal title. In the wake of *Gladstone*, the range of legislative objectives that can justify the infringement of aboriginal title is fairly broad. Most of these objectives can be traced to the *reconciliation* of the prior occupation of North America by aboriginal peoples with the assertion of Crown sovereignty, which entails the recognition that "distinctive aboriginal societies exist within, and are a part of, a broader social, political and economic community" (at para. 73). In my opinion, the development of agriculture, forestry, mining, and hydroelectric power, the general economic development of the interior of British Columbia, protection of the environment or endangered species, the building of infrastructure and the settlement of foreign populations to support those aims, are the kinds of objectives that are

consistent with this purpose and, in principle, can justify the infringement of aboriginal title. Whether a particular measure or government act can be explained by reference to one of those objectives, however, is ultimately a question of fact that will have to be examined on a case-by-case basis.

166 The manner in which the fiduciary duty operates with respect to the second stage of the justification test—both with respect to the standard of scrutiny and the particular form that the fiduciary duty will take—will be a function of the nature of aboriginal title. Three aspects of aboriginal title are relevant here. First, aboriginal title encompasses the right to *exclusive* use and occupation of land; second, aboriginal title encompasses *the right to choose* to what uses land can be put, subject to the ultimate limit that those uses cannot destroy the ability of the land to sustain future generations of aboriginal peoples; and third, that lands held pursuant to aboriginal title have an inescapable economic component.

167 The exclusive nature of aboriginal title is relevant to the degree of scrutiny of the infringing measure or action. For example, if the Crown's fiduciary duty requires that aboriginal title be given priority, then it is the altered approach to priority that I laid down in *Gladstone* which should apply. What is required is that the government demonstrate (at para. 62) "both that the process by which it allocated the resource and the actual allocation of the resource which results from that process reflect the prior interest" of the holders of aboriginal title in the land. By analogy with *Gladstone*, this might entail, for example, that governments accommodate the participation of aboriginal peoples in the development of the resources of British Columbia, that the conferral of fee simples for agriculture, and of leases and licences for forestry and mining reflect the prior occupation of aboriginal title lands, that economic barriers to aboriginal uses of their lands (e.g., licensing fees) be somewhat reduced. This list is illustrative and not exhaustive. This is an issue that may involve an assessment of the various interests at stake in the resources in question. No doubt, there will be difficulties in determining the precise value of the aboriginal interest in the land and any grants, leases or licences

given for its exploitation. These difficult economic considerations obviously cannot be solved here.

168 Moreover, the other aspects of aboriginal title suggest that the fiduciary duty may be articulated in a manner different than the idea of priority. This point becomes clear from a comparison between aboriginal title and the aboriginal right to fish for food in *Sparrow*. First, aboriginal title encompasses within it a right to choose to what ends a piece of land can be put. The aboriginal right to fish for food, by contrast, does not contain within it the same discretionary component. This aspect of aboriginal title suggests that the fiduciary relationship between the Crown and aboriginal peoples may be satisfied by the involvement of aboriginal peoples in decisions taken with respect to their lands. There is always a duty of consultation. Whether the aboriginal group has been consulted is relevant to determining whether the infringement of aboriginal title is justified, in the same way that the Crown's failure to consult an aboriginal group with respect to the terms by which reserve land is leased may breach its fiduciary duty at common law: *Guerin*. The nature and scope of the duty of consultation will vary with the circumstances. In occasional cases, when the breach is less serious or relatively minor, it will be no more than a duty to discuss important decisions that will be taken with respect to lands held pursuant to aboriginal title. Of course, even in these rare cases when the minimum acceptable standard is consultation, this consultation must be in good faith, and with the intention of substantially addressing the concerns of the aboriginal peoples whose lands are at issue. In most cases, it will be significantly deeper than mere consultation. Some cases may even require the full consent of an aboriginal nation, particularly when provinces enact hunting and fishing regulations in relation to aboriginal lands.

169 Second, aboriginal title, unlike the aboriginal right to fish for food, has an inescapably economic aspect, particularly when one takes into account the modern uses to which lands held pursuant to aboriginal title can be put. The economic aspect of aboriginal title suggests that compensation is relevant to the question of justification as well, a possibility suggested in *Sparrow* and

which I repeated in *Gladstone*. Indeed, compensation for breaches of fiduciary duty are a well-established part of the landscape of aboriginal rights: *Guerin*. In keeping with the duty of honour and good faith on the Crown, fair compensation will ordinarily be required when aboriginal title is infringed. The amount of compensation payable will vary with the nature of the particular aboriginal title affected and with the nature and severity of the infringement and the extent to which aboriginal interests were accommodated. Since the issue of damages was severed from the principal action, we received no submissions on the appropriate legal principles that would be relevant to determining the appropriate level of compensation of infringements of aboriginal title. In the circumstances, it is best that we leave those difficult questions to another day.

D. *Has a Claim to Self-government Been Made out by the Appellants?*

170 In the courts below, considerable attention was given to the question of whether s. 35(1) can protect a right to self-government, and if so, what the contours of that right are. The errors of fact made by the trial judge, and the resultant need for a new trial, make it impossible for this Court to determine whether the claim to self-government has been made out. Moreover, this is not the right case for the Court to lay down the legal principles to guide future litigation. The parties seem to have acknowledged this point, perhaps implicitly, by giving the arguments on self-government much less weight on appeal. One source of the decreased emphasis on the right to self-government on appeal is this Court's judgment in *Pamajewon*. There, I held that rights to self-government, if they existed, cannot be framed in excessively general terms. The appellants did not have the benefit of my judgment at trial. Unsurprisingly, as counsel for the Wet'suwet'en specifically concedes, the appellants advanced the right to self-government in very broad terms, and therefore in a manner not cognizable under s. 35(1).

171 The broad nature of the claim at trial also led to a failure by the parties to address many of the difficult conceptual issues which surround the recognition of aboriginal self-government.

The degree of complexity involved can be gleaned from the *Report of the Royal Commission on Aboriginal Peoples*, which devotes 277 pages to the issue. That report describes different models of self-government, each differing with respect to their conception of territory, citizenship, jurisdiction, internal government organization, etc. We received little in the way of submissions that would help us to grapple with these difficult and central issues. Without assistance from the parties, it would be imprudent for the Court to step into the breach. In these circumstances, the issue of self-government will fail to be determined at trial.

E. *Did the Province Have the Power to Extinguish Aboriginal Rights After 1871, Either Under its Own Jurisdiction or Through the Operation of s. 88 of the Indian Act?*

(1) *Introduction*

172 For aboriginal rights to be recognized and affirmed by s. 35(1), they must have existed in 1982. Rights which were extinguished by the sovereign before that time are not revived by the provision. In a federal system such as Canada's, the need to determine whether aboriginal rights have been extinguished raises the question of which level of government has jurisdiction to do so. In the context of this appeal, that general question becomes three specific ones. First, there is the question whether the province of British Columbia, from the time it joined Confederation in 1871, until the entrenchment of s. 35(1) in 1982, had the jurisdiction to extinguish the rights of aboriginal peoples, including aboriginal title, in that province. Second, if the province was without such jurisdiction, another question arises—whether provincial laws which were not in pith and substance aimed at the extinguishment of aboriginal rights could have done so nevertheless if they were laws of general application. The third and final question is whether a provincial law, which could otherwise not extinguish aboriginal rights, be given that effect through referential incorporation by s. 88 of the *Indian Act*.

(2) *Primary Jurisdiction*

173 Since 1871, the exclusive power to legislate in relation to

"Indians, and Lands reserved for the Indians" has been vested with the federal government by virtue of s. 91(24) of the *Constitution Act, 1867*. That head of jurisdiction, in my opinion, encompasses within it the exclusive power to extinguish aboriginal rights, including aboriginal title.

(a) "Lands reserved for the Indians"

174 I consider the second part of this provision first, which confers jurisdiction to the federal government over "Lands reserved for the Indians". The debate between the parties centred on whether that part of s. 91(24) confers jurisdiction to legislate with respect to aboriginal title. The province's principal submission is that "Lands reserved for the Indians" are lands which have been specifically set aside or designated for Indian occupation, such as reserves. However, I must reject that submission, because it flies in the face of the judgment of the Privy Council in *St. Catherine's Milling*. One of the issues in that appeal was the federal jurisdiction to accept the surrender of lands held pursuant to aboriginal title. It was argued that the federal government, at most, had jurisdiction over "Indian Reserves". Lord Watson, speaking for the Privy Council, rejected this argument, stating that had the intention been to restrict s. 91(24) in this way, specific language to this effect would have been used. He accordingly held that (at p. 59):

the words actually used are, according to their natural meaning, sufficient to include all lands reserved, upon any terms or conditions, for Indian occupation.

Lord Watson's reference to "all lands" encompasses not only reserve lands, but lands held pursuant to aboriginal title as well. Section 91(24), in other words, carries with it the jurisdiction to legislate in relation to aboriginal title. It follows, by implication, that it also confers the jurisdiction to extinguish that title.

175 The province responds by pointing to the fact that underlying title to lands held pursuant to aboriginal title vested with the provincial Crown pursuant to s. 109 of the *Constitution Act, 1867*. In its submission, this right of ownership carried with it the right to grant fee simples which, by implication, extinguish aboriginal

title, and so by negative implication excludes aboriginal title from the scope of s. 91(24). The difficulty with the province's submission is that it fails to take account of the language of s. 109, which states in part that:

All Lands, Mines, Minerals, and Royalties belonging to the several Provinces of Canada ... at the Union ... shall belong to the several Provinces ... subject to any Trusts existing in respect thereof, and to any Interest other than that of the Province in the same.

Although that provision vests underlying title in provincial Crowns, it qualifies provincial ownership by making it subject to the "any Interest other than that of the Province in the same". In *St. Catherine's Milling*, the Privy Council held that aboriginal title was such an interest, and rejected the argument that provincial ownership operated as a limit on federal jurisdiction. The net effect of that decision, therefore, was to separate the ownership of lands held pursuant to aboriginal title from jurisdiction over those lands. Thus, although on surrender of aboriginal title the province would take absolute title, jurisdiction to accept surrenders lies with the federal government. The same can be said of extinguishment—although on extinguishment of aboriginal title, the province would take complete title to the land, the jurisdiction to extinguish lies with the federal government.

176 I conclude with two remarks. First, even if the point were not settled, I would have come to the same conclusion. The judges in the court below noted that separating federal jurisdiction over Indians from jurisdiction over their lands would have a most unfortunate result—the government vested with primary constitutional responsibility for securing the welfare of Canada's aboriginal peoples would find itself unable to safeguard one of the most central of native interests—their interest in their lands. Second, although the submissions of the parties and my analysis have focussed on the question of jurisdiction over aboriginal title, in my opinion, the same reasoning applies to jurisdiction over any aboriginal right which relates to land. As I explained earlier, *Adams* clearly establishes that aboriginal rights may be tied to land but

nevertheless fall short of title. Those relationships with the land, however, may be equally fundamental to aboriginal peoples and, for the same reason that jurisdiction over aboriginal title must vest with the federal government, so too must the power to legislate in relation to other aboriginal rights in relation to land.

(b) "Indians"

177 The extent of federal jurisdiction over Indians has not been definitively addressed by this Court. We have not needed to do so because the *vires* of federal legislation with respect to Indians, under the division of powers, has never been at issue. The cases which have come before the Court under s. 91(24) have implicated the question of jurisdiction over Indians from the other direction —whether provincial laws which on their face apply to Indians intrude on federal jurisdiction and are inapplicable to Indians to the extent of that intrusion. As I explain below, the Court has held that s. 91(24) protects a "core" of Indianness from provincial intrusion, through the doctrine of interjurisdictional immunity.

178 It follows, at the very least, that this core falls within the scope of federal jurisdiction over Indians. That core, for reasons I will develop, encompasses aboriginal rights, including the rights that are recognized and affirmed by s. 35(1). Laws which purport to extinguish those rights therefore touch the core of Indianness which lies at the heart of s. 91(24), and are beyond the legislative competence of the provinces to enact. The core of Indianness encompasses the whole range of aboriginal rights that are protected by s. 35(1). Those rights include rights in relation to land; that part of the core derives from s. 91(24)'s reference to "Lands reserved for the Indians". But those rights also encompass practices, customs and traditions which are not tied to land as well; that part of the core can be traced to federal jurisdiction over "Indians". Provincial governments are prevented from legislating in relation to both types of aboriginal rights.

(3) *Provincial Laws of General Application*

179 The vesting of exclusive jurisdiction with the federal government over Indians and Indian lands under s. 91(24), operates to

preclude provincial laws in relation to those matters. Thus, provincial laws which single out Indians for special treatment are *ultra vires*, because they are in relation to Indians and therefore invade federal jurisdiction: see *R. v. Sutherland*, [1980] 2 S.C.R. 451. However, it is a well-established principle (quoting from *Four B Manufacturing Ltd.*, *supra*, at p. 1048) that:

> The conferring upon Parliament of exclusive legislative competence to make laws relating to certain classes of persons does not mean that the totality of these persons' rights and duties comes under primary federal competence to the exclusion of provincial laws of general application.

In other words, notwithstanding s. 91(24), provincial laws of general application apply *proprio vigore* to Indians and Indian lands. Thus, this Court has held that provincial labour relations legislation (*Four B*) and motor vehicle laws (*R. v. Francis*, [1988] 1 S.C.R. 1025), which purport to apply to all persons in the province, also apply to Indians living on reserves.

180 What must be answered, however, is whether the same principle allows provincial laws of general application to extinguish aboriginal rights. I have come to the conclusion that a provincial law of general application could not have this effect, for two reasons. First, a law of general application cannot, by definition, meet the standard which has been set by this Court for the extinguishment of aboriginal rights without being *ultra vires* the province. That standard was laid down in *Sparrow*, *supra*, at p. 1099, as one of "clear and plain" intent. In that decision, the Court drew a distinction between laws which extinguished aboriginal rights, and those which merely regulated them. Although the latter types of laws may have been "necessarily inconsistent" with the continued exercise of aboriginal rights, they could not extinguish those rights. While the requirement of clear and plain intent does not, perhaps, require that the Crown "use language which refers expressly to its extinguishment of aboriginal rights" (*Gladstone*, *supra*, at para. 34), the standard is still quite high. My concern is that the only laws with the sufficiently clear and plain intention to extinguish aboriginal rights would be laws in

relation to Indians and Indian lands. As a result, a provincial law could never, *proprio vigore*, extinguish aboriginal rights, because the intention to do so would take the law outside provincial jurisdiction.

181 Second, as I mentioned earlier, s. 91(24) protects a core of federal jurisdiction even from provincial laws of general application, through the operation of the doctrine of interjurisdictional immunity. That core has been described as matters touching on "Indianness" or the "core of Indianness" (*Dick, supra,* at pp. 326 and 315; also see *Four B, supra,* at p. 1047 and *Francis, supra,* at pp. 1028–29). The core of Indianness at the heart of s. 91(24) has been defined in both negative and positive terms. Negatively, it has been held to not include labour relations (*Four B*) and the driving of motor vehicles (*Francis*). The only positive formulation of Indianness was offered in *Dick.* Speaking for the Court, Beetz J. assumed, but did not decide, that a provincial hunting law did not apply *proprio vigore* to the members of an Indian band to hunt and because those activities were "at the centre of what they do and what they are" (at p. 320). But in *Van der Peet,* I described and defined the aboriginal rights that are recognized and affirmed by s. 35(1) in a similar fashion, as protecting the occupation of land and the activities which are integral to the distinctive aboriginal culture of the group claiming the right. It follows that aboriginal rights are part of the core of Indianness at the heart of s. 91(24). Prior to 1982, as a result, they could not be extinguished by provincial laws of general application.

(4) *Section 88 of the Indian Act*

182 Provincial laws which would otherwise not apply to Indians *proprio vigore,* however, are allowed to do so by s. 88 of the *Indian Act,* which incorporates by reference provincial laws of general application: *Dick, supra,* at pp. 326–27; *Derrickson v. Derrickson,* [1986] 1 S.C.R. 285, at p. 297; *Francis, supra,* at pp. 1030–31. However, it is important to note, in Professor Hogg's words, that s. 88 does not "invigorate" provincial laws which are invalid because they are in relation to Indians and Indian lands (*Constitutional Law of Canada* (3rd ed. 1992), at p. 676; also see *Dick, supra,* at

p. 322). What this means is that s. 88 extends the effect of provincial laws of general application which cannot apply to Indians and Indian lands because they touch on the Indianness at the core of s. 91(24). For example, a provincial law which regulated hunting may very well touch on this core. Although such a law would not apply to aboriginal people *proprio vigore*, it would still apply through s. 88 of the *Indian Act*, being a law of general application. Such laws are enacted to conserve game and for the safety of all.

183 The respondent B.C. Crown argues that since such laws are *intra vires* the province, and applicable to aboriginal persons, s. 88 could allow provincial laws to extinguish aboriginal rights. I reject this submission, for the simple reason that s. 88 does not evince the requisite clear and plain intent to extinguish aboriginal rights. The provision states in full:

Subject to the terms of any treaty and any other Act of Parliament, all laws of general application from time to time in force in any province are applicable to and in respect of Indians in the province, except to the extent that those laws are inconsistent with this Act or any order, rule, regulation or by-law made thereunder, and except to the extent that those laws make provision for any matter for which provision is made by or under this Act.

I see nothing in the language of the provision which even suggests the intention to extinguish aboriginal rights. Indeed, the explicit reference to treaty rights in s. 88 suggests that the provision was clearly not intended to undermine aboriginal rights.

VI. Conclusion and Disposition

184 For the reasons I have given above, I would allow the appeal in part, and dismiss the cross-appeal. Reluctantly, I would also order a new trial.

185 I conclude with two observations. The first is that many aboriginal nations with territorial claims that overlap with those of the appellants did not intervene in this appeal, and do not appear to have done so at trial. This is unfortunate, because determinations of aboriginal title for the Gitksan and Wet'suwet'en will undoubtedly affect their claims as well. This is particularly

so because aboriginal title encompasses an *exclusive* right to the
use and occupation of land, i.e., to the *exclusion* of both non-
aboriginals and members of other aboriginal nations. It may,
therefore, be advisable if those aboriginal nations intervened in
any new litigation.

186 Finally, this litigation has been both long and expensive,
not only in economic but in human terms as well. By ordering a
new trial, I do not necessarily encourage the parties to proceed to
litigation and to settle their dispute through the courts. As was
said in *Sparrow, supra*, at p. 1105, s. 35(1) "provides a solid constitutional base upon which subsequent negotiations can take place".
Those negotiations should also include other aboriginal nations
which have a stake in the territory claimed. Moreover, the Crown
is under a moral, if not a legal, duty to enter into and conduct
those negotiations in good faith. Ultimately, it is through negotiated settlements, with good faith and give and take on all sides,
reinforced by the judgments of this Court, that we will achieve
what I stated in *Van der Peet, supra*, at para. 31, to be a basic
purpose of s. 35(1)—"the reconciliation of the pre-existence of
aboriginal societies with the sovereignty of the Crown". Let us
face it, we are all here to stay.

The reasons of La Forest and L'Heureux-Dubé JJ. were delivered by

LA FOREST J.

187 I have read the reasons of the Chief Justice, and while I
agree with his conclusion, I disagree with various aspects of his
reasons and in particular, with the methodology he uses to prove
that aboriginal peoples have a general right of occupation of certain lands (often referred to as "aboriginal title").

188 I begin by considering why a new trial is necessary in this
case. It is true, as the Chief Justice points out, that the amalgamation of the appellants' individual claims represents a defect in
the pleadings and, technically speaking, this prevents us from
considering the merits of the case. However, in my view, there is
a more substantive problem with the pleadings in this case. Before
this Court, the appellants sought a declaration of "aboriginal title"

but attempted, in essence, to prove that they had complete control over the territory in question. The appellants effectively argued on appeal, as they did at trial, that by virtue of their social and land tenure systems—consisting of Chief authority, Houses, feasts, crests, and totem poles—they acquired an absolute interest in the claimed territory, including ownership of and jurisdiction over the land. The problem with this approach is that it requires proof of governance and control as opposed to proof of general occupation of the affected land. Only the latter is the *sine qua non* of "aboriginal title". It follows that what the appellants sought by way of declaration from this Court and what they set out to prove by way of the evidence were two different matters. In light of this substantive defect in the pleadings, a new trial should be ordered to permit a reassessment of the matter on the basis of these reasons.

189 In my view, the foundation of "aboriginal title" was succinctly described by Judson J. in *Calder v. Attorney-General of British Columbia*, [1973] S.C.R. 313, where, at p. 328, he stated: "the fact is that when the settlers came, the Indians were there, organized in societies and occupying the land as their forefathers had done for centuries. This is what Indian title means". Relying in part on Judson J.'s remarks, Dickson J. (as he then was) wrote in *Guerin v. The Queen*, [1984] 2 S.C.R. 335, at p. 382, that aboriginal peoples have a "legal right to occupy and possess certain lands, the ultimate title to which is in the Crown". As well, in *Canadian Pacific Ltd. v. Paul*, [1988] 2 S.C.R. 654, this Court stated, at p. 678: "The inescapable conclusion from the Court's analysis of Indian title up to this point is that the Indian interest in land is truly *sui generis*. It is more than the right to enjoyment and occupancy although ... it is difficult to describe what more in traditional property law terminology". More recently, Judson J.'s views were reiterated in *R. v. Van der Peet*, [1996] 2 S.C.R. 507. There Lamer C.J. wrote for the majority, at para. 30, that the doctrine of aboriginal rights (one aspect of which is "aboriginal title") arises from "one simple fact: when Europeans arrived in North America, aboriginal peoples *were already here*, living in communities on the land, and participating in distinctive cultures, as they had done for centuries" (emphasis in original).

190 It follows from these cases that the aboriginal right of possession is derived from the historic occupation and use of ancestral lands by aboriginal peoples. Put another way, "aboriginal title" is based on the continued occupation and use of the land as part of the aboriginal peoples' traditional way of life. This *sui generis* interest is not equated with fee simple ownership; nor can it be described with reference to traditional property law concepts. The best description of "aboriginal title", as set out above, is a broad and general one derived from Judson J.'s pronouncements in *Calder, supra*. Adopting the same approach, Dickson J. wrote in *Guerin, supra*, that the aboriginal right of occupancy is further characterized by two principal features. First, this *sui generis* interest in the land is personal in that it is generally inalienable except to the Crown. Second, in dealing with this interest, the Crown is subject to a fiduciary obligation to treat aboriginal peoples fairly. Dickson J. went on to conclude, at p. 382, that "[a]ny description of Indian title which goes beyond these two features is both unnecessary and potentially misleading". I share his views and am therefore reluctant to define more precisely the "right [of aboriginal peoples] to continue to live on their lands as their forefathers had lived"; see *Calder*, at p. 328.

191 The approach I adopt, in defining the aboriginal right of occupancy, is also a highly contextual one. More specifically, I find it necessary to make a distinction between: (1) the recognition of a general right to occupy and possess ancestral lands; and (2) the recognition of a discrete right to engage in an aboriginal activity in a particular area. I defined the latter in *R. v. Côté*, [1996] 3 S.C.R. 139, at para. 97, as "the traditional use, by a tribe of Indians, that has continued from pre-contact times of a particular area for a particular purpose". The issue in *Côté*, as in *Van der Peet*, was whether the use of a particular fishing spot was really an aspect of the aboriginal peoples' way of life in pre-contact times; see also in the *Van der Peet* trilogy *R. v. Gladstone*, [1996] 2 S.C.R. 723, and *R. v. N.T.C. Smokehouse Ltd.*, [1996] 2 S.C.R. 672. In all those cases, the fishing rights asserted by the aboriginal claimants were not associated with a more general occupancy of the affected land. By contrast, the present case deals with a general claim to occupy

and possess vast tracts of territory (58,000 square kilometres). This type of generalized land claim is not merely a bundle of discrete aboriginal rights to engage in specific activities. Rather, it is, as the Chief Justice states, at para. III, the "right to use land for a variety of activities, not all of which need be aspects of practices, customs and traditions which are integral to the distinctive cultures of aboriginal societies". These land-based activities are, of course, related to the aboriginal society's habits and mode of life.

192 I note, as well, that in defining the nature of "aboriginal title", one should generally not be concerned with statutory provisions and regulations dealing with reserve lands. In *Guerin, supra*, this Court held that the interest of an Indian band in a reserve is derived from, and is of the same nature as, the interest of an aboriginal society in its traditional tribal lands. Accordingly, the Court treated the aboriginal interest in reserve lands as one of occupation and possession while recognizing that the underlying title to those lands was in the Crown. It was not decided in *Guerin, supra*, and it by no means follows, that specific statutory provisions governing reserve lands should automatically apply to traditional tribal lands. For this reason, I am unable to assume that specific "reserve" provisions of the *Indian Act*, R.S.C., 1985, c. I-5, and the *Indian Oil and Gas Act*, R.S.C., 1985, c. I-7, apply to huge tracts of land which are subject to an aboriginal right of occupancy.

193 I turn next to this Court's decision in *Van der Peet, supra*, where the Chief Justice identified a number of factors essential to the recognition of aboriginal rights under s. 35(1) of the *Constitution Act, 1982*. As I have already indicated, the *Van der Peet* trilogy dealt with activity-based discrete rights and, more specifically, with fishing activities that were carried out in the face of statutory prohibitions. By contrast, the present case deals with a generalized claim over vast tracts of territory, a claim which is itself the foundation for particular rights and activities. Moreover, I agree with the appellants that this generalized claim should not be defined as merely a compendium of aboriginal rights, each of which must meet the test set out in *Van der Peet*. Nonetheless, I am of the view that the "key" factors identified in *Van der Peet*, namely precision,

specificity, continuity, and centrality are still met by my approach in the present case.

194 First, it is clear that the nature of an aboriginal claim must be identified *precisely* with regard to particular practices, customs and traditions. As already mentioned, when dealing with a claim of "aboriginal title", the court will focus on the occupation and use of the land as part of the aboriginal society's *traditional way of life*. In pragmatic terms, this means looking at the manner in which the society used the land *to live*, namely to establish villages, to work, to get to work, to hunt, to travel to hunting grounds, to fish, to get to fishing pools, to conduct religious rites, etc. These uses, although limited to the aboriginal society's traditional way of life, may be exercised in a contemporary manner; see *R. v. Sparrow*, [1990] 1 S.C.R. 1075, at p. 1099.

195 Second, it is self-evident that an aboriginal society asserting the right to live on its ancestral lands must *specify* the area which has been continuously used and occupied. That is, the general boundaries of the occupied territory should be identified. I recognize, however, that when dealing with vast tracts of territory it may be impossible to identify geographical limits with scientific precision. Nonetheless, this should not preclude the recognition of a general right of occupation of the affected land. Rather, the drawing of exact territorial limits can be settled by subsequent negotiations between the aboriginal claimants and the government.

196 Some would also argue that specificity requires *exclusive* occupation and use of the land by the aboriginal group in question. The way I see it, exclusivity means that an aboriginal group must show that a claimed territory is indeed *its* ancestral territory and not the territory of an unconnected aboriginal society. On the other hand, I recognize the possibility that two or more aboriginal groups may have occupied the same territory and used the land communally as part of their traditional way of life. In cases where two or more groups have accommodated each other in this way, I would not preclude a finding of joint occupancy. The result may be different, however, in cases where one dominant aboriginal group has merely permitted other groups to use the territory

or where definite boundaries were established and maintained between two aboriginal groups in the same territory.

197 Third, as indicated above, the aboriginal right of possession is based on the *continued* occupation and use of traditional tribal lands. The Chief Justice concludes that the relevant time period for the establishment of "aboriginal title" is the time at which the Crown asserted sovereignty over the affected land. I agree that in the context of generalized land claims, it is more appropriate, from a practical and theoretical standpoint, to consider the time of sovereignty as opposed to the time of first contact between an aboriginal society and Europeans. However, I am also of the view that the date of sovereignty may not be the only relevant moment to consider. For instance, there may have been aboriginal settlements in one area of the province but, after the assertion of sovereignty, the aboriginal peoples may have all moved to another area where they remained from the date of sovereignty until the present. This relocation may have been due to natural causes, such as the flooding of villages, or to clashes with European settlers. In these circumstances, I would not deny the existence of "aboriginal title" in that area merely because the relocation occurred post-sovereignty. In other words, continuity may still exist where the present occupation of one area is connected to the pre-sovereignty occupation of another area.

198 Also, on the view I take of continuity, I agree with the Chief Justice that it is not necessary for courts to have conclusive evidence of pre-sovereignty occupation. Rather, aboriginal peoples claiming a right of possession may provide evidence of present occupation as proof of prior occupation. Further, I agree that there is no need to establish an unbroken chain of continuity and that interruptions in occupancy or use do not necessarily preclude a finding of "title". I would go further, however, and suggest that the presence of two or more aboriginal groups in a territory may also have an impact on continuity of use. For instance, one aboriginal group may have ceded its possession to subsequent occupants or merged its territory with that of another aboriginal society. As well, the occupancy of one aboriginal society may be connected to the occupancy of another society by conquest or

exchange. In these circumstances, continuity of use and occupation, extending back to the relevant time, may very well be established; see Brian Slattery, "Understanding Aboriginal Rights" (1987), 66 *Can. Bar Rev.* 727, at p. 759.

199 Fourth, if aboriginal peoples continue to occupy and use the land as part of their traditional way of life, it necessarily follows that the land is of *central significance* to them. As already suggested, aboriginal occupancy refers not only to the presence of aboriginal peoples in villages or permanently settled areas. Rather, the use of adjacent lands and even remote territories to pursue a traditional mode of life is also related to the notion of occupancy. Viewed in this light, occupancy is part of aboriginal culture in a broad sense and is, therefore, absorbed in the notion of distinctiveness. To use the language of *Van der Peet*, proof of occupancy is proof of centrality.

200 I would also add that my approach regarding the nature of aboriginal occupancy is supported by the terms of the *Royal Proclamation, 1763*, R.S.C., 1985, App. II, No. 1. Although the *Proclamation* is not the sole source of "aboriginal title" in this country, it bears witness to the British policy towards aboriginal peoples which was based on respect for their right to occupy their ancestral lands; see *Sparrow, supra*, at p. 1103. Specifically, the *Proclamation* provides:

And We do further declare it to be Our Royal Will and Pleasure, for the present as aforesaid, to reserve under our Sovereignty, Protection, and Dominion, for the use of the said Indians, all the Lands and Territories not included within the Limits of Our said Three new Governments, or within the Limits of the Territory granted to the Hudson's Bay Company, as also all the Lands and Territories lying to the Westward of the Sources of the Rivers which fall into the Sea from the West and North West as aforesaid.

In clear terms vast tracts of territory (including large portions of the area now comprising Ontario, Quebec, and the prairie provinces) were reserved for aboriginal peoples. These huge tracts of land were by no means limited to villages or permanent settlements but were reserved more generally as "Hunting Grounds" and "for the use of the said Indians". Aboriginal peoples had the right to possess the lands reserved for them and "not be molested or disturbed in the Possession" of such territory. In essence, the rights set out in the *Proclamation*—which were applied in principle to aboriginal peoples across the country—underlie the view I have taken of aboriginal occupancy; see *R. v. Wesley*, [1932] 4 D.L.R. 774 (Alta. S.C., App. Div.), at p. 787, and *R. v. Sikyea* (1964), 43 D.L.R. (2d) 150 (N.W.T.C.A.), aff'd *Sikyea v. The Queen*, [1964] S.C.R. 642.

201 The analysis thus far has focussed on the nature of the aboriginal right to occupy and possess certain lands—a right recognized and affirmed under s. 35(1) of the *Constitution Act, 1982*. Nonetheless, as Dickson C.J. and I wrote in *Sparrow, supra*, at p. 1109: "Rights that are recognized and affirmed are not absolute". Thus, government regulation can infringe upon aboriginal rights if it meets the test of justification under s. 35(1). It is important to emphasize as well that the approach adopted under s. 35(1) is a highly contextual one. This is also clear from the reasons I wrote jointly with Dickson C.J. in *Sparrow*, at p. 1111:

> We wish to emphasize the importance of context and a case-by-case approach to s. 35(1). Given the generality of the text of the constitutional provision, and especially in light of the complexities of aboriginal history, society and rights, the contours of a justificatory standard must be defined in the specific factual context of each case.

202 In the context of the present case, I agree with the Chief Justice that the general economic development of the interior of British Columbia, through agriculture, mining, forestry, and hydroelectric power, as well as the related building of infrastructure and settlement of foreign populations are valid legislative objectives that, in principle, satisfy the first part of the justification analysis.

203 Under the second part of the justification test, these legislative objectives are subject to accommodation of the aboriginal peoples' interests. This accommodation must always be in accordance with the honour and good faith of the Crown. Moreover, when dealing with a generalized claim over vast tracts of land, accommodation is not a simple matter of asking whether licences have been fairly allocated in one industry, or whether conservation

measures have been properly implemented for a specific resource. Rather, the question of accommodation of "aboriginal title" is much broader than this. Certainly, one aspect of accommodation in this context entails notifying and consulting aboriginal peoples with respect to the development of the affected territory. Another aspect of accommodation is fair compensation. More specifically, in a situation of expropriation, one asks whether fair compensation is available to the aboriginal peoples; see *Sparrow*, *supra*, at p. 1119. Indeed, the treatment of "aboriginal title" as a compensable right can be traced back to the *Royal Proclamation, 1763*. The relevant portions of the *Proclamation* are as follows:

such Parts of Our Dominions and Territories as, not having been ceded to or purchased by Us, are reserved to them [aboriginal peoples] or any of them, as their Hunting Grounds.

. . .

We do, with the Advice of our Privy Council strictly enjoin and require, that no private Person do presume to make any purchase from the said Indians of any Lands reserved to the said Indians . . . but that, if at any Time any of the Said Indians should be inclined to dispose of the said Lands, the same shall be Purchased only for Us, in our Name.

Clearly, the *Proclamation* contemplated that aboriginal peoples would be compensated for the surrender of their lands; see also Slattery, "Understanding Aboriginal Rights", *supra*, at pp. 751–52. It must be emphasized, nonetheless, that fair compensation in the present context is not equated with the price of a fee simple. Rather, compensation must be viewed in terms of the right and in keeping with the honour of the Crown. Thus, generally speaking, compensation may be greater where the expropriation relates to a village area as opposed to a remotely visited area. I add that account must be taken of the interdependence of traditional uses to which the land was put.

204 In summary, in developing vast tracts of land, the government is expected to consider the economic well being of *all* Canadians. But the aboriginal peoples must not be forgotten in this equation. Their legal right to occupy and possess certain lands, as confirmed by s. 35(1) of the *Constitution Act, 1982*, mandates

basic fairness commensurate with the honour and good faith of the Crown.

205 With regard to the issue of self-government, I conclude, as does the Chief Justice, that there was insufficient evidence before this Court to make any determination regarding this aspect of the appellants' claim.

206 As for the issue raised on the cross-appeal, I agree with the Chief Justice's conclusion. The respondent province had no authority to extinguish aboriginal rights either under the *Constitution Act, 1867* or by virtue of s. 88 of the *Indian Act*.

207 On a final note, I wish to emphasize that the best approach in these types of cases is a process of negotiation and reconciliation that properly considers the complex and competing interests at stake. This point was made by Lambert J.A. in the Court of Appeal, [1993] 5 W.W.R. 97, at pp. 379–80:

So, in the end, the legal rights of the Indian people will have to be accommodated within our total society by political compromises and accommodations based in the first instance on negotiation and agreement and ultimately in accordance with the sovereign will of the community as a whole. The legal rights of the Gitksan and Wet'suwet'en peoples, to which this law suit is confined, and which allow no room for any approach other than the application of the law itself, and the legal rights of all aboriginal peoples throughout British Columbia, form only one factor in the ultimate determination of what kind of community we are going to have in British Columbia and throughout Canada in the years ahead.

(See also *Report of the Royal Commission on Aboriginal Peoples* (1996), vol. 2 (*Restructuring the Relationship*), Part 2, at pp. 561–62.)

208 Accordingly, I would allow the appeal in part and order a new trial on the basis of the principles set out in these reasons. I would also dismiss the cross-appeal.

The following are the reasons delivered by

MCLACHLIN J.

209 I concur with the Chief Justice. I add that I am also in substantial agreement with the comments of Justice La Forest.

SCHEDULE 1

Appellants

DELGAMUUKW, also known as Earl Muldoe, suing on his own behalf and on behalf of all the members of the Houses of Delgamuukw and Haaxw

GISDAY WA, also known as Alfred Joseph, suing on his own behalf and on behalf of all the members of the House of Gisday Wa

NII KYAP, also known as Gerald Gunanoot, suing on his own behalf and on behalf of all the members of the House of Nii Kyap

LELT, also known as Lloyd Ryan, suing on his own behalf and on behalf of all the members of the Houses of Lelt and Haak'w

ANTGULILBIX, also known as Mary Johnson, suing on her own behalf and on behalf of all the members of the House of Antgulilbix

TENIMGYET, also known as Arthur Matthews, Jr., suing on his own behalf and on behalf of all the members of the House of Tenimgyet

GOOHLAHT, also known as Lucy Namox, suing on her own behalf and on behalf of all the members of the Houses of Goohlaht and Samooh

KLIIYEM LAX HAA, also known as Eva Sampson, suing on her own behalf and on behalf of all the members of the Houses of Kliiyem Lax Haa and Wii'mugulsxw

GWIS GYEN, also known as Stanley Williams, suing on his own behalf and on behalf of all the members of the House of Gwis Gyen

KWEESE, also known as Florence Hall, suing on her own behalf and on behalf of all the members of the House of Kweese

DJOGASLEE, also known as Walter Wilson, suing on his own behalf and on behalf of all the members of the House of Djogaslee

GWAGL'LO, also known as Ernest Hyzims, suing on his own behalf and on behalf of all the members of the Houses of Gwagl'lo and Duubisxw

GYOLUGYET, also known as Mary McKenzie, suing on her own behalf and on behalf of all the members of the House of Gyolugyet

GYETM GALDOO, also known as Sylvester Green, suing on his own behalf and on behalf of all the members of the Houses of Gyetm Galdoo and Wii'Goob'l

HAAK ASXW, also known as Larry Wright, suing on his own behalf and on behalf of all the members of the House of Haak Asxw

GEEL, also known as Walter Harris, suing on his own behalf and on behalf of all the members of the House of Geel

HAALUS, also known as Billy Morrison, suing on his own behalf and on behalf of all the members of the House of Haalus

WII HLENGWAX, also known as Herbert Burke, suing on his own behalf and on behalf of all the members of the House of Wii Hlengwax

LUUTKUDZIIWUS, also known as Ben McKenzie, Sr., suing on his own behalf and on behalf of all the members of the House of Luutkudziiwus

MA'UUS, also known as Jeffrey Harris, Jr., suing on his own behalf and on behalf of all the members of the House of Ma'uus

MILUU LAK, also known as Alice Jeffery, suing on her own behalf and on behalf of all the members of the Houses of Miluu Lak and Haiwas

NIKA TEEN, also known as James Woods, suing on his own behalf and on behalf of all the members of the House of Nika Teen

SKIIK'M LAX HA, also known as John Wilson, suing on his own behalf and on behalf of all the members of the House of Skiik'm Lax Ha

WII MINOSIK, also known as Robert Stevens, suing on his own behalf and on behalf of all the members of the House of Wii Minosik

GWININ NITXW, also known as Solomon Jack, suing on his own behalf and on behalf of all the members of the House of Gwinin Nitxw

GWOIMT, also known as Kathleen Wale, suing on her own behalf and on behalf of all the members of the Houses of Gwoimt and Tsabux

LUUS, also known as Jeffrey Harris, suing on his own behalf and on behalf of all the members of the House of Luus

NIIST, also known as David Blackwater, suing on his own behalf and on behalf of all the members of the Houses of Niist and Baskyelaxha

SPOOKW, also known as Steven Robinson, suing on his own behalf and on behalf of all the members of the Houses of Spookw and Yagosip

WII GAAK, also known as Neil Sterritt, Sr., suing on his own behalf and on behalf of all the members of the House of Wii Gaak

DAWAMUXW, also known as Charlie Clifford, suing on his own behalf and on behalf of all the members of the House of Dawamuxw

GITLUDAHL, also known as Peter Muldoe, suing on his own behalf and on behalf of all the members of the Houses of Gitludahl and Wiigyet

GUXSAN, also known as Herbert Wesley, suing on his own behalf and on behalf of all the members of the House of Guxsan

HANAMUXW, also known as Joan Ryan, suing on her own behalf and on behalf of all the members of the House of Hanamuxw

YAL, also known as George Turner, suing on his own behalf and on behalf of all the members of the House of Yal

GWIIYEEHL, also known as Chris Skulsh, suing on his own behalf and on behalf of all the members of the House of Gwiiyeehl

SAKXUM HIGOOKX, also known as Vernon Smith, suing on his own behalf and on behalf of all the members of the House of Sakxum Higookx

MA DEEK, also known as James Brown, suing on his own behalf and on behalf of all the members of the House of Ma Deek

WOOS, also known as Roy Morris, suing on his own behalf and on behalf of all the members of the House of Woos

KNEDEBEAS, also known as Sarah Layton, suing on her own behalf and on behalf of all the members of the House of Knedebeas

SMOGELGEM, also known as Leonard George, suing on his own behalf and on behalf of all the members of the House of Smogelgem

KLO UM KHUN, also known as Patrick Pierre, suing on his own behalf and on behalf of all the members of the House of Klo Um Khun

HAG WIL NEGH, also known as Ron Mitchell, suing on his own behalf and on behalf of all the members of the House of Hag Wil Negh

WAH TAH KEG'HT, also known as Henry Alfred, suing on his own behalf and on behalf of all the members of the House of Wah Tah Keg'ht

WAH TAH KWETS, also known as John Namox, suing on his own behalf and on behalf of all the members of the House of Wah Tah Kwets

WOOSIMLAXHA, also known as Victor Mowatt, suing on his own behalf and on behalf of all the members of the House of Gutginuxw

XSGOGIMLAXHA, also known as Vernon Milton, suing on his own behalf and on behalf of all the members of the House of Xsgogimlaxha

WIIGYET, also known as Roy Wesley, suing on his own behalf and on behalf of all the members of the House of Wiigyet

WII ELAAST, also known as Jim Angus, Jr., suing on his own behalf and on behalf of all the members of the Houses of Wii Elaast and Amagyet

GAXSBGABAXS, also known as Gertie Watson, suing on her own behalf and on behalf of all the members of the House of Gaxsbgabaxs

WIGETIMSCHOL, also known as Dan Michell, suing on his own behalf and on behalf of all the members of the House of Namox

SCHEDULE 2

Those Intervening with the Musqueam Nation

Delbert Guerin

Gail Y. Sparrow

Jim Kew

Larry Grant

Leona M. Sparrow

Mary Charles

Myrtle McKay

Nolan Charles

Susan A. Point

Chief George Guerin

SCHEDULE 3

Those Intervening with the B.C. Cattlemen's Association

B.C. Chamber of Commerce

B.C. Wildlife Federation

Business Council of British Columbia

Council of Tourist Associations

Fisheries Council of British Columbia

Guideoutfitters Association of British Columbia

Mining Association of British Columbia

Pacific Fishermen's Defence Alliance

Appeal allowed in part; cross-appeal dismissed.

Solicitors for the appellants and respondents on the cross-appeal, the Gitksan Hereditary Chiefs et al.: Rush, Crane, Guenther & Adams, Vancouver.

Solicitors for the appellants and respondents on the cross-appeal, the Wet'suwet'en Hereditary Chiefs et al.: Blake, Cassels & Graydon, Vancouver.

Solicitors for the respondent and appellant on the cross-appeal, Her Majesty the Queen in Right of the Province of British Columbia: Arvay, Finlay, Victoria.

Solicitor for the respondent the Attorney General of Canada: The Attorney General of Canada, Ottawa.

Solicitors for the intervener the First Nations Summit: Ratcliff & Company, North Vancouver.

Solicitors for the intervener the Westbank First Nation: Woodward and Company, Victoria.

Solicitors for the interveners the Musqueam Nation et al.: Blake, Cassels & Graydon, Vancouver.

Solicitor for the interveners the B.C. Cattlemen's Association, et al.: J. Keith Lowes, Vancouver.

Solicitors for the intervener Skeena Cellulose Inc.: Russell & DuMoulin, Vancouver.

Solicitors for the intervener Alcan Aluminum Ltd.: Lawson, Lundell, Lawson & McIntosh, Vancouver.

NOTE: Sopinka J. [listed as present on p. 25] took no part in this judgment.

©CRDP 1996

The official version may be found in the Supreme Court Reports.

THE DAVID SUZUKI FOUNDATION: WORKING TOGETHER FOR A SUSTAINABLE FUTURE

The David Suzuki Foundation was established to work for a world of hope in which our species thrives in balance with the productive capacity of the Earth.

Our mission is to find solutions to the root causes of our most threatening environmental problems. Then, we work with our supporters and their communities to implement those solutions for a sustainable future.

Our mandate is broad, ranging from projects on climate change, air, soil, water, fisheries, forestry, energy, and liveable cities, to defining the foundations of sustainability, how social change occurs, and the potential of new economic models.

We can only accomplish this with the support of concerned citizens who care about the environment. We invite your help.

JOIN OUR PARTNERSHIP ... JOIN THE FOUNDATION

To find out how you can become a Friend of the Foundation or to make a donation, contact:

THE DAVID SUZUKI FOUNDATION
219–2211 WEST FOURTH AVENUE
VANCOUVER, B.C., CANADA V6K 4S2
Phone (604) 732-4228; Fax (604) 732-0752

Charitable Registration Nos. Canada: 0873299-52, U.S.: 94-3204049

Thank you very much for your support!